Drawing Inferences from Self-Selected Samp

Drawing Inferences from Self-Selected Samples

Edited by
Howard Wainer

With 17 Figures

LEA LAWRENCE ERLBAUM ASSOCIATES, PUBLISHERS
Mahwah, New Jersey

Howard Wainer
Educational Testing Service
Research Statistics Group
Princeton, New Jersey 08541

Originally published in 1986.

Lawrence Erlbaum Associates, Inc., Publishers
10 Industrial Avenue
Mahwah, New Jersey 07430

Library of Congress Cataloging-in-Publication Data

Drawing inferences from self-selected samples.
  Papers from a conference sponsored by
  Educational Testing Service.
  Includes bibliographical references and index.
  ISBN 0-8058-3802-3
  1. Social sciences–Statistical methods.
2. Sampling (Statistics). 3. Educational Statistics.
I. Wainer, Howard. II Educational Testing Service.
HA31.2.D7 1986   519.5'2   86-15593

Printed in the United States of America

10 9 8 7 6 5 4 3 2 1

To Henry and Paul

From left to right: John Tukey, Donald Rubin, Burton Singer, Robert Glynn, Howard Wainer, John Hartigan

Preface

During the course of the rhetoric surrounding the 1984 Presidential election campaign in the United States there were a variety of statements made that gave me pause. For example, I heard candidate Ferraro explain her poor showing in pre-election polls by saying, "I don't believe those polls. If you could see the enthusiasm for our candidacy 'out there' you wouldn't believe them either." Obviously, trying to estimate one's popularity in the entire voting population from the enthusiasm of your supporters at political rallies is not likely to yield accurate results. I suspect that trying to statistically adjust the "rally estimate" through the use of the demographic characteristics of those who attend would not have helped enough to be useful. A modest survey on a more randomly chosen sample would surely have been better.

At about the same time, Secretary of Education Terrell Bell released a table entitled *State Education Statistics*. Among other bits of information, it contained the mean scores on the Scholastic Aptitude Test (the SAT) for 22 of the states. The College Board had previously released these mean scores for all states. At this point the mass media began carrying reports interpreting the differences.

The Reagan White House pointed out that spending more money on education was not the way to improve educational outcomes. To support this they pointed to the mean SAT scores of Connecticut and New Hampshire. New Hampshire had modestly higher SAT scores but lower "per pupil expenditure."

When the SAT scores halted their 15-year decline and began to rise, the Reagan White House hinted that this happy occurrence was due to the no-nonsense view that the administration had taken toward education. Former Commissioner of Education, Harold Howe, had a different view. He pointed out that the turnaround might in fact be due to Reagan policies, but not in the way that the White House would have us believe.

> ...what President Reagan did was remove the low-scoring group from test taking by reducing the federal loans and grants that make it possible for them

to go to college. As he reduced these funds, students from poor families
...stopped taking the SAT.... These shifts in the plans of students removed
a group of low scores from test taking and raised the average of those who did
take the test. The President's contribution to improving education is analogous to the initiatives some high schools take to persuade teenagers to drop
out of school before the annual competency test rolls around. Then the
average of those remaining goes up and everybody feels good about the
school. Such practices constitute a powerful new weapon for improving
education by raising scores. (Howe, 1984)

Howe's interpretation, though consistent with the data, is not the only
one possible. It does point out that when one is trying to draw valid
generalizations from self-selected samples, disagreements are likely to arise.
Obviously the characteristics that one observes in self-selected populations
need to be dealt with before drawing any, even temporary, conclusions. It
was clear to even a lay observer that some sort of statistical adjustment was
required. But what sort?

In November of 1984, the *Harvard Educational Review* published a paper
by two educational researchers (Powell and Steelman, 1984) which proposed a method of covariance adjustment for these SAT data. This was
hailed as an important step by no less a statistical expert than Albert
Shanker (*New York Times*, January 6, 1985), the president of the American
Federation of Teachers.

The success that Powell and Steelman met with in adjusting SAT scores
came as some surprise to me, especially since we at ETS had been trying to
work out a reasonable way to accomplish exactly the same thing for some
time. Our conclusion (Wainer et al., 1985) was that the traditional *pro
forma* methods of adjustment were not up to the task. Could we have been
too dense? Or perhaps too pessimistic?

I was torn in two directions. First, I remembered Cochran's famous
example of how trying to adjust oat yields after fumigation by the size of
the remaining eelworm population was almost surely the wrong way to go.
This was reinforced by my colleague Paul Rosenbaum's conclusion that,
"Estimators that adjust for a concomitant variable that has been affected
by the treatment are generally biased." (Rosenbaum, 1984, p. 656). It
seemed clear to me that adjusting for selection by using "percentage of high
school seniors in a state who took the SAT" as a covariate would encounter
this pitfall.

But countering this was the knowledge of our everyday behavior. For
example, we often make decisions that a restaurant is no good on the basis
of a single meal. We don't randomly sample around the menu, we may not
try it on a Thursday, and we don't adjust for time of day nor month of the
year. Yet we live with these decisions, and if by chance we resample, we are
not often surprised. Could it be that adjusting in a way that is statistically
naive and formally incorrect might still yield useful results?

At the same time that I was worrying about this, Paul Holland asked if I would organize the 1985 ETS "Statistics Day." This is ETS's annual conference which was originally conceived of as providing an opportunity for local statisticians to meet with outstanding colleagues and to take part in discussions of important statistical topics in congenial surroundings. My initial reaction was to reject this since I had more than enough professional activities to fully occupy my onrushing middle years. Then an idea struck—suppose I could organize "Statistics Day" around a common theme and invite the best people I could find to come and discuss that topic? The idea of using this vehicle to try to get a better handle on how we can draw inferences from self-selected samples once established became irresistible. Unfortunately, since the original goals of "Statistics Day" were much more modest, the budget originally allocated by ETS for this activity would not support what I wanted to do.

At this point entrepreneurial optimism took over. I telephoned a number of talented friends who have interests in this area and explained my idea. Don Rubin, who is perhaps the foremost scholar in this area, agreed to come and talk about some new ideas on which he and his colleagues had been working. He suggested that Burt Singer had some self-selection problems which might be interesting to hear about. Burt also agreed to come. I called John Hartigan, who had discussed this topic with me during a visit I made to Yale the previous year. I thought that at last I might be able to get him to provide further details of a scheme he had previously inscribed with his finger on the frosted window of his wife's Datsun. He told me that since the thaw he had nothing new to say, but that he was quite interested in what others might say, and would serve as a discussant.

Next I called John Tukey. My previous experience with John has taught me many things; one of them is that he is a compulsive problem-solver. Gordon Sande once said of him that, "For any given problem John can immediately offer seven solutions. Two can be dismissed after a few minutes thought, two can be dismissed after working on them for a couple of months, and the remaining three will be right on." My own observations confirm Sande's, although John has denied this, saying that he is usually content if he can come up with just one workable solution. My expectations were high that we would come out with something if only I could convince John to participate. Fortunately the topic interested him and his schedule allowed his attendance. I was elated when he agreed to be a discussant.

Tradition and time constraints dictated having four papers. With Rubin and Singer we were halfway there. Jim Heckman was next. I knew of Jim's work on selection modeling and had heard of some interesting confrontations he and Don Rubin had had on this topic during the time they had both been at Chicago. This seemed like a good opportunity to get to hear them face-to-face. After some effort I succeeded in tracking Jim down at his Yale office (quite a commute from his Chicago home) and asked if he would come and tell us how he thought selection modeling—currently in vogue in econometrics—might help out in this problem. Happily, he too agreed. With this lineup of home run hitters I justified my own position on the program on the grounds that they needed a lead-off batter to get on base and start the rally.

The lineup thus worked out, I wrote a short proposal to NSF to fund the conference. It was my great good fortune that Murray Aborn and Sara Beth Nerlove shared my enthusiasm for both the importance of the topic and the strength of the program. They moved the proposal through the NSF review procedures with an alacrity that I had not thought possible. I thank them and the National Science Foundation (Grant #SES-8505591 to the Educational Testing Service) for making this possible.

At the same time that Aborn and Nerlove were working their Washington miracle, Ernie Anastasio (then Vice President of Research of ETS), Henry Braun (Division Director of Statistical Analysis at ETS), and Paul Holland (Director of the Research Statistics Group) were working to assure ETS's support. Because of their joint efforts all the pieces were put into place to get 1985's "Statistics Day" off the ground. We had the talent and the money. The only thing lacking was the organizational sweat. This was provided first by Vera House and later by Linda DeLauro. Linda wrote letters, arranged travel, reserved rooms, planned menus, cajoled, and coerced. Afterwards, she transcribed the lively discussion into textual form. Having listened carefully to the taped transcripts myself during the course of editing the discussions, I have great appreciation for the dedication that this took.

In addition to those previously mentioned I would like to thank Sharon Stewart and Kathy Fairall for their invaluable help in the myriad of clerical tasks required to get tidy manuscripts ready for publication. Also, to the staff of the Henry Chauncey Conference Center for the help they provided in the smooth running of the conference.

Contents

List of Contributors

ROBERT J. GLYNN
Massachusetts Eye and Ear Infirmatory, Boston, MA

JOHN HARTIGAN
Yale University, New Haven, CT

JAMES J. HECKMAN
University of Chicago, Chicago, IL

PAUL W. HOLLAND
Educational Testing Service, Princeton, NJ

NAN M. LAIRD
Harvard University, Cambridge, MA

RICHARD ROBB
The Chicago Corporation, Chicago, IL

DONALD B. RUBIN
Harvard University, Cambridge, MA

BURTON SINGER
Yale University, New Haven, CT

JOHN W. TUKEY
Princeton University, Princeton, NJ

HOWARD WAINER
Educational Testing Service, Princeton, NJ

Introduction
and Overview

HOWARD WAINER

This volume grew out of a multiplicity of concerns about the use of self-selected samples to draw causal inferences. Singer's concern showed itself in the study of the efficacy of various drug rehabilitation programs; Heckman and Robb's in studying the worth of job training programs; Glynn, Laird, and Rubin's in a comparison of alcohol consumption level of two groups of individuals. John Tukey is interested in most things; if you can get his attention you will always depart wiser than when you arrived.

My own particular interest was in the use of college entrance exams as indicants of the performance of state educational systems. The most obvious manifestation of this has become the Department of Education's annual unveiling of the "Wall Chart" entitled *State Education Statistics*, which began in 1984 and is in its third incarnation as we go to press. In this compendium the principal indicators of state performance are the mean scores for the SAT (the College Board's Scholastic Aptitude Test) or the ACT (American College Testing program). These are generated by a self-selected sample of students who are considering enrollment in colleges that require such scores.

Inferences about these scores are of two general types:

(1) *tracking the same group over time* (e.g., "Blacks have improved 9 points since last year."; or "The overall score decline which begin in 1963 has ended this year as scores went up 2 points."; or "New Jersey's scores went up."); and

(2) *comparing subgroups at the same time* (e.g., "New Hampshire had higher mean SAT scores than did Connecticut").

In addition, various combinations of these were common (e.g., "Minority performance in New Jersey improved more sharply over the last two years than it did in New York."). Response to these sorts of statements was quick —especially from states with lower scores. Often this was of the form "A greater proportion of students in our state take the SAT" or "We have a different ethnic/economic mix than do other states." These responses are quite justified, and social scientists with access to computers and regression programs immediately jumped in with the intention of helping policy makers (see, e.g., Powell and Steelman, 1984; Steelman and Powell, 1985; Page and Feifs, 1985). This "help" took the form of new tables which contained adjusted state rankings. The adjustments were done by hypothesizing (either implicitly or explicitly) some model of participation and covarying out whatever was on hand that might plausibly measure the variable of interest in the model. Also used as covariates were those background variables that made direct comparisons unfair.

In addition to studies that adjusted state test scores were others that criticized such adjustments as being flawed conceptually, statistically, and/or epistemologically (Wainer et al., 1985; Wainer, 1986). While such criticisms are valuable in pointing out what we cannot do, it does not help policy makers who look toward the scientific community for advice in their difficult tasks. Later in this volume John Tukey refers to two kinds of lawyers–one who tells you that something can't be done and the other who tells you how to do it; he clearly views the latter as the correct attitude. This volume is a first step toward an understanding of these problems and their eventual solution.

The first chapter ("The SAT as a Social Indicator: A Pretty Bad Idea," by Wainer) describes in greater detail why one might want to draw inferences from college entrance exams and points out some of the problems involved in the current approaches. It provides evidence that simple participation models (higher ability students are more likely to take college entrance exams) are not true enough to be useful for the sorts of fine distinctions that policy makers wish to make. It suggests that equating rather than regression adjustments ought to be considered and that survey information, which does not suffer from the same problems of self-selection, ought to be used. It concludes that with current data sources and simple covariance adjustments, the results available are too coarse for serious work.

The second chapter ("Self-Selection and Performance-Based Ratings: A Case Study in Program Evaluation," by Singer) presents a history of Methadone Maintenance Treatments. The evaluation of such programs contains many of the same problems involved in the college entrance exam situation. The key element is self-selection. Singer describes details of a number of such programs around the world and draws conclusions based upon gross similarities. He suggests that simple models don't work and that comparisons of relative efficacy can only be made approximately. In his words, we can

> only focus on coarse features of clinics and the patient population. Indeed, it is only at this coarse level that meaningful program evaluation can be carried out.... Any more refined comparisons would either require unrealistically large numbers of clinics or strong modeling assumptions which, for the present, could not be easily defended.

The third chapter ("Alternative Methods for Solving the Problem of Selection Bias in Evaluating the Impact of Treatments on Outcomes," by Heckman and Robb) provides a description of one methodology—selection modeling—to begin to deal with these problems. This methodology, reduced to its simplest form, consists of four steps:

(1) *observe* the distribution of the outcome variables of interest;
(2) *hypothesize* the functional relationship between the likelihood of participation and the variables observed;
(3) *believe* the selection model assumed in step (2); and
(4) *calculate* the distribution of the outcome variables for both those who are observed and those who are not.

Rubin, in his presentation, pointed out that step (3) was the most difficult step. The ease with which Heckman accomplishes this apparently led both Tukey and Hartigan to suggest (implicitly) that perhaps this step is easier for economists than for statisticians.

Heckman and Robb's chapter differs from the others in this volume in another important way. *It was not what was presented at the conference.* The paper that was presented ("Alternative Methods for Evaluating the Impact of Interventions") was published in 1985 in *Longitudinal Analysis of Labor Market Data* (Heckman and Singer, eds., New York: Cambridge University Press). The comments of the discussants were on the presented paper and not on the one published here. The version contained here responded to some of the criticisms of the discussants. To preserve the chronology of events, we first present the discussion of the original paper (interested readers can go to the above source), then the revised version, and finally John Tukey's comments on the revised manuscript. John Hartigan declined comment on the revision.

The last chapter ("Selection Modeling versus Mixture Modeling with Nonignorable Nonresponse," by Glynn, Laird, and Rubin) compares the

selection modeling approach with Rubin's (1977) method of mixture modeling. The distinction between these two methods can be most precisely and
compactly stated mathematically. Moreover, I believe that understanding
will be facilitated if both the general idea of these methods and the notation
that the authors have used is familiar to the reader. Let me briefly describe
them.

Definitions:

> Y is a variable of interest, taking values y
> R indicates if a unit has responded ($R = 1$) or hasn't ($R = 0$).

We are interested in the joint distribution of Y and R over the entire
population of interest. The first two steps of selection modeling can be
denoted then as:

(1) *observe* the distribution of $Y|R = 1$, and then
(2) *hypothesize* the probability of $R = 1 | Y = y$.

It is useful to state the probability of $R = 1 | Y = y$ explicitly. It is,

$$\frac{\text{number of respondents at } Y = y}{(\text{number of respondents at } Y = y) + (\text{number of nonrespondents at } Y = y)}.$$

Note that the numerator is known, but that the denominator is made up of
two terms. The first is known, the second is unknowable.

In mixture modeling we note that there are two distributions of interest:
the distribution of $Y|R = 1$ and $Y|R = 0$. The first of these conditional
distributions is observed; the second is not. Nothing we do can change this
basic fact. The first two steps in mixture modeling, comparable to those in
selection modeling are

(1) *observe* the distribution of $Y|R = 1$, and then
(2) *hypothesize* the distribution of $Y|R = 0$.

One next mixes them properly and outputs a result. Glynn et al. then
integrate this notion with Rubin's (1978) scheme of multiple imputation* in
which a (possibly wide) variety of possible step (2)'s are imputed, each
yielding a different result. The variation of the results yielded by a variety
of imputed distributions of $Y|R = 0$ conveys the range of variation of result
of our current state of knowledge.

As Hartigan points out in his discussion of the Glynn et al. paper, these
two approaches (except for the emphasis on multiple imputation) are just
two sides of the same joint distribution. The essential difference (see
Holland's comment following the last chapter) is that mixture modeling

---

*Tukey feels that this would be better termed "parallel" or "repeated" imputation. Although
we agree with the distinction that this terminologic change suggests, we will continue to use
"multiple" to maintain congruence with Glynn et al.

makes it unambiguously clear what is known and what is unknown, whereas selection modeling stirs the two together.

The unanimous conclusion of our conference was that simple covariance adjustments of the sort in common use today can almost surely be improved upon. These improvements are most obvious in the assessment of uncertainty that such schemes as multiple imputation provide. Moreover at least one observer (John Tukey) felt that he was "moderately convinced that this is the state-of-the-art." This will be of scant help to the policy maker who notes that his state has rather different rankings depending upon whose adjustment he uses and wants to know which one is right. Using newer methodology, he will probably discover that neither was right and that the two different results are merely symptoms of the underlying uncertainty of result implicit in our ignorance of the self-selection process.

Bibliography

Heckman, J.J. and Robb, R. (1985). "Alternative methods for evaluating the impact of interventions," In J. Heckman and B. Singer (eds.), *Longitudinal Analysis of Labor Market Data*. New York: Cambridge University Press, Chapt. 4, pp. 156–245.

Page, E.B. and Feifs, H. (1985). "SAT scores and American states: Seeking for useful meaning." *J. Ed. Meas.*, 22, 305–312.

Powell, B. and Steelman, L.C. (1984). "Variations in state SAT performance: Meaningful or misleading?" *Harvard Ed. Rev.*, 54, 389–412.

Rubin, D.B. (1977). "Formalizing subjective notions about the effect of nonrespondents in sample surveys." *J. Amer. Statist. Assoc.*, 72, 538–543.

Rubin, D.B. (1978). "Multiple imputations in sample surveys—A phenomenological Bayesian approach to nonresponse." In *Imputation and Editing of Faulty or Missing Data*. Washington, D.C.: U.S. Department of Commerce, Social Security Administration, pp. 1–18.

Steelman, L.C. and Powell, B. (1985). "Appraising the implications of the SAT for educational policy." *Phi Delta Kappan*, 603–606.

Wainer, H. (1986). "Five pitfalls encountered while trying to compare states on their SAT scores." *J. Ed. Meas.*, 23, 69–81.

Wainer, H., Holland, P.W., Swinton, S., and Wang, M. (1985). "On 'State Education Statistics'." *J. Ed. Statist.*, 10, 293–325.

The SAT as a Social Indicator:
A Pretty Bad Idea*

HOWARD WAINER

I. Introduction

The effort expended in the gathering, analyzing, and disseminating of educational data on a national level has waxed and waned since the 1867 establishment of a federal agency for these purposes. The issues which prompted the 1866–1867 Congressional debates—fear of federal control of education, state, and local accountability for expenditure of federal funds and quality of data collected at the national level—are still with us. Events such as the launching of Sputnik in 1957 and the report by the National Commission on Excellence in Education 1983 yielded increased public attention to the performance of the educational system.

A variety of data gathering efforts have been instituted at the Federal level over the last 20 years to:

(1) account for the use of federal funds by states and localities,
(2) measure the progress toward national goals such as compensatory education and education of the handicapped,
(3) show what techniques and practices were successful, and
(4) monitor compliance with civil rights statutes.

In January 1984 the Secretary of Education released a chart entitled *State Education Statistics* that compared the 50 states and the District of Columbia on a number of educational variables for the years 1972 and 1982. The outcome variables that received the greatest public attention were each state's average SAT (Scholastic Aptitude Test) or ACT (American College Testing program) score.

The construction of this chart is but one instance of the common practice of using standardized test scores in general, and SAT scores in particular, as indicators of educational attainment.

---

*This paper was presented as part of the Educational Testing Service "Statistics Day" on April 27, 1985. It draws heavily from the earlier work (Wainer *et al.*, 1985) that was done in collaboration with Paul Holland, Paul Rosenbaum, Spencer Swinton, and Minhwei Wang.

The SAT is used this way primarily because it is

(1) highly visible,
(2) carefully equated and thus has (more than other tests) the same meaning from year to year, and
(3) taken by very large numbers of individuals.

Yet, how valid is the use of the SAT as a social indicator? Can we infer educational trends from SAT trends? Are they a useful measure for such purposes as the four mentioned previously?

In this paper we would like to consider the use of the SAT as a social indicator for two separate but related purposes. The first is to track national educational trends in performance. The second is to study the effects of variations in educational policy, techniques, and practices that are visible as "natural experiments" within definable groups of SAT test takers.

These applications share a common problem: unwanted variation in other variables which affect (bias) the dependent variable measured—the SAT score. In the first application, which involves tracking national trends, variations in the make-up of the group who elect to take the SAT over the period being studied can have profound effects. We cannot merely look at the raw mean SAT score and derive meaningful inferences: some sorts of adjustment must be made. The most obvious variation that has occurred in the SAT-taking population over the past two decades has been the increasing percentage of high school age students who take it. More subtle are the variations in the demographic make-up of this increased market share.

The second application, which involves studying variation in educational policy through the "natural variation" observed in subgroups of SAT takers, shares this problem. In this instance we might group states (or some other unit) by some theoretically manipulatable variable (e.g., per pupil expenditure), to try to answer the question, "Does spending more on each student improve performance?" Yet, if the states included in these groups vary on other uncontrolled factors (e.g., percent participation, parental education, racial composition), are our comparisons valid? Once again, before we can draw inferences from this natural experiment, we must somehow adjust for the unintended differences in the states.

This paper deals with the differences that are seen among the states that make these kinds of comparisons difficult and with an approach to the problem of statistical adjustment. We discuss some of the previous approaches to the statistical adjustment of these data and point out their shortcomings. We conclude that none of the methods so far utilized to solve this problem resolve the self-selection difficulties sufficiently for practical purposes. The evidence so far available indicates that when decisions of importance need to be made from variables requiring statistical adjustment, one must, at some time, for some subset of the observations, do it right—i.e., get a random sample. Random samples are required to check on

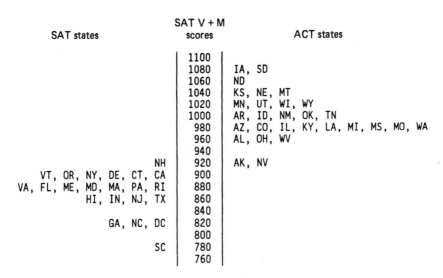

Figure 1. SAT total (verbal + mathematics) scores for 1981–1982 for SAT and ACT states.

the accuracy of the adjustment scheme. One cannot merely adjust without checking and announce that "the experimental units are now comparable."

II. The Problem of Self-Selection

The Scholastic Aptitude Test (SAT) is given in all 50 states and the District of Columbia. In 21 states and the District of Columbia (what we shall term the "SAT states"), a majority of the students who take any college entrance exam take the SAT. In 28 of the remaining states the majority of these students take a roughly comparable exam given by the American College Testing program (ACT). In the remaining state, Washington, a majority do not take either exam, but many take the ACT. We shall refer to these 29 states as the "ACT states."

Shown in Figure 1 is a back-to-back inside-out plot of the average SAT scores for all 51 "states," each classified as an SAT state or an ACT state (data from the College Entrance Examination Board). From this plot we might conclude that:

(1) students in the ACT states are better at taking the SAT than those in the SAT states, or

(2) those in the ACT states who choose to take the SAT are a more select group than in the SAT states.

10   Howard Wainer

```
                          Rank
        SAT states       (% ile)          ACT states
                           91   | SD
                           90   | IA, ND
                           89   | AR
                           88   | MS, NE, NV, WY
                           87   | ID, KS, KY, MT, OK, UT, WV
                           86   |
                           84   | AL, AZ, NM, WI
                           83   | LA, MN, TN, WA
                           82   | CO, MI
                           81   | MO
                           80   | AK, OH
                    OR     79   | IL
                    CA     78   |
                           77   |
                VT, TX     76   |
            NC, ME, FL     75   |
        SC, NH, IN, GA     74   |
                    PA     73   |
                VA, MN     72   |
            RI, DC, DE     71   |
    NY, NJ, MA, HI, CT     70   |
```

Figure 2. Mean rank in class (percentile) for those taking SAT.

There is ample support for the latter hypothesis. For example, Figure 2 shows the mean rank in class (self-reported from Education Testing Service Student Descriptive Questionnaires, or SDQ) for students taking the SAT in each state. We see that almost all ACT states report that their average SAT candidates are in the top 20% of their class. No SAT state is in this range. In Figure 3 is shown a display of parental income (also from the SDQ) which indicates a similar disparity between the distributions of SAT and ACT states.

Is It Just the Selection Ratio?

Can we account for the unusual success enjoyed by the ACT state candidates on the SAT by merely pointing to the smaller selection ratio? I suspect not. Consider for a moment the data shown in Figure 4, which indicates the relationship between the percentage of high school students taking the ACT in 1972 and in 1982 in the ACT states. Note the position of Nebraska. It had the largest change in percentage participation on the ACT of all ACT states, going from 29% in 1972 to 73% in 1982. Ordinarily, with such a vast rise in participation rate, we would expect a decline in mean performance. In fact (see Figure 5), there was a decline in performance for all ACT states during this decade, but Nebraska's was among the smallest! Subsequent investigations showed that during this time period (1976), the University of Nebraska changed its admission standards to require the

SAT states	Income ($ X 1000)	ACT states
	49	AK
	48	
	47	
	46	LA, OK
	45	IL, MN
	44	KS
	43	
	42	CO, IA, MI, ND, TN, UT
	41	WY
	40	AL, AZ, KY, MS, MO
	39	NM, WI
TX, MD	38	OH, WA
CA	37	AR, NE
VA, CT	36	ID, NV, WV
DC, DE	35	
NJ	34	SD
HI, FL	33	MT
OR	32	
NH, GA	31	
MA, IN	30	
PA, NY	29	
NC	28	
VT, RI	27	
SC	26	
ME	25	

Figure 3. Mean parental income per state for students who take the SAT (in thousands of dollars).

ACT of all applicants. Thus, many of the students who represent the increase in the ACT participation rate had previously taken the SAT. This group is typically (in ACT states at least) of higher ability and so the average performance did not suffer as one might have suspected given the increase in participation rate. This is meant to illustrate that something else is going on besides just rate changes. One must also consider changes in the internal criteria that students use when they decide to take one entrance exam or another.

The strong relationship between the participation rate and performance on the SAT has not gone unnoticed by contemporary investigators (see Powell and Steelman, 1984; Page and Feifs, 1985). A common tactic used to correct for this is to covary out the participation rate. Powell and Steelman (1984) conclude that about 82% of the variation in states' performance can be attributed to this variable and that "at best, only 18 percent can be considered 'real' variation" (p. 400). Is this true? Can some "real" variation be masked by the percentage of participation? Does this adjustment miss anything having to do with *who* decides to take the SAT, rather than merely *how many* decide to take it? Is this adjustment adding bias to the results?

Suppose we consider the set of natural experiments for which the SAT score might be a plausible outcome variable. In many of these the treatment

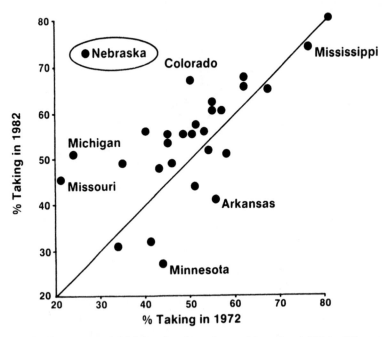

Figure 4. Percentage of high school seniors taking the ACT in 28 states in 1972 and in 1982.

could be bound up with the quality of the school system. It is well established that higher quality schools will yield a greater proportion of their graduates to the SAT-taking pool (at least in SAT states). Furthermore, the percentage taking the SAT from a state is highly correlatable with the average SAT score in that state. Thus, "percentage taking the SAT" can be thought of as a posttreatment concomitant variable. We know (Rosenbaum, 1984, p. 656) that, "estimators that adjust for a concomitant variable that has been affected by the treatment are generally biased."

The classic example of this was provided by Cochran (1957). He described an agricultural experiment in which various oat fields were either fumigated or not according to some experimental design. The fumigation was to rid the field of eelworms. There were two outcome variables: number of eelworms left and yield of oats. An overzealous analyst, after noting that the fumigation was differentially effective (as measured by the number of eelworms left), might decide to "improve" precision by measuring oat fields *after* adjusting for number of eelworms. In this instance "number of eelworms" is a posttreatment concomitant variable. One obvious interpretation of these results is that when eelworms are fewer, oat yields are larger; but if we adjust away the effect of the eelworms, this disappears and also might the effect of the treatment.

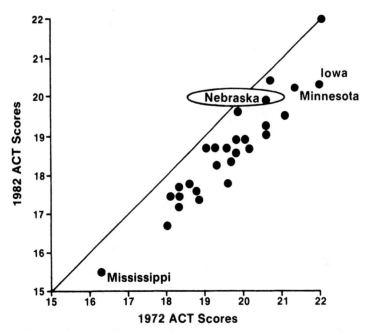

Figure 5. Mean ACT scores in 28 states in 1972 and in 1982.

In the current situation it seems clear that "percentage taking the SAT" can be considered as a posttreatment concomitant variable, and adjusting for it seems at the onset to be fraught with difficulties. One plausible alternative is to reduce the size of the selection effect by enlarging the SAT pool. This is especially important in the ACT states if we wish to compare SAT states with ACT states. This seems doable if mean ACT scores can be equated to some SAT equivalent.

Such a task has been attempted by a number of researchers, and a summary of some of these is shown in Figure 6. The three studies (Astin, 1971; Chase and Barrett, 1966; Pugh and Sassenrath, 1968) shown use different methods, but arrive at encouragingly similar results for the range of scores of interest (for ACT scores between 15 and 25). A linear transformation of ACT to SAT scores (SAT = 40 ACT + 110) can be used to enlarge the examinee sample. When we use this transformation in the ACT states to obtain an SAT mean score for the majority of students and then combine this with those who actually took the SAT, we obtain an estimated SAT mean score for each ACT state based upon all students who took either entrance exam. In SAT states the proportions taking the ACT are too small to have an effect on the overall mean and we used just the SAT scores to represent the state. A back-to-back inside-out plot with the

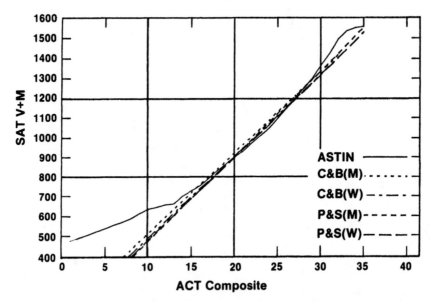

Figure 6. Published studies on corresponding SAT verbal and mathematics scores. Astin indicates the Astin (1971) study; C&B, the Chase and Barrett (1966) study; and P&S, the Pugh and Sassenrath (1968) study. Results for men (M) and women (W) are shown separately.

results of this is shown in Figure 7. Contrast these results with those shown in Figure 1.

These modified results are closer to our expectations than those which included only SAT takers. The median score for ACT states is the same as for SAT states; geographically and economically similar states group together. It is instructive to compare these results, based upon all of the test takers, to those obtained by Powell and Steelman (1984) who tried to use a statistical adjustment on the results of only a (sometimes) small percentage of the test takers. This comparison is shown graphically in Figure 8. Two characteristics are immediately evident. First, we see that there are substantial deviations from a perfect linear relationship. These deviations range up to about 50 SAT points. If we assume that the ACT–SAT concatenation is the more accurate representation, then these deviations represent a shortfall of the covariance strategy. I believe that this is a reasonable inference.

The second aspect of interest in this display is that the greater the amount of adjustment required, the greater the error. This is not a surprising result. We can deduce this by examining the different regression lines that are associated with the SAT states (relatively steep) and the ACT states (relatively shallow). Although the differences between these two regression lines are exacerbated by some fringelying points, there remain real differences.

SAT states		Scores	ACT states
		950	MN, WI
		940	
	NH	930	IA
		920	CO, NE
	OR	910	MT
VT, NY, DE, CT,	CA	900	AK, OH, WY
VA, MA, MD, ME,	FL	890	AZ, MI, MO
RI,	PA	880	ID, IL, KS, SD
TX,	NJ	870	
IN,	HI	860	NV, UT
		850	
		840	NM, OK, TN, WV
	NC	830	AR, KY, ND
DC,	GA	820	AL
		810	
		800	LA
	SC	790	
		780	
		770	
		760	
		750	
		740	MS

Figure 7. SAT total (verbal + mathematics) scores concatenated with transformed ACT scores.

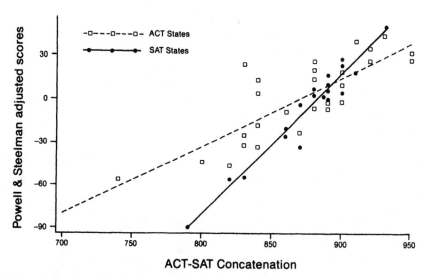

Figure 8. A graphical comparison between Powell and Steelman (1984) adjusted SAT scores and the results of the ACT–SAT concatenation.

This exercise provides us with an important lesson. We ought to not merely do a covariance adjustment and declare the problem solved. We need to check the results, to whatever extent possible, against the true state of affairs. Often this latter state is not available; if it was, why would we bother trying to adjust to it? But often we can approximate it, at least for a subset of the population of interest. In this instance, although we could not estimate the SAT scores for all of the high school population, we could do it for a much larger portion than just the SAT takers. When we did this, we found that the covariance adjustment was moving in the right direction, but was far from perfect. How accurate need the adjustment be for us to conclude that it is accurate enough for our purpose? Obviously this question does not admit to a general answer, for it depends on the situation. But we can put residuals of 50 SAT points into a context. Consider that the SAT score decline, a topic of national attention, averaged about 3 SAT points per year for 15 years. Thus, this entire decline, 45 points, would be within the margin of adjustment error. We conclude that for purposes of tracking national and state trends, this adjustment is too inaccurate for our purpose.

III. Further Adjustments and Inferences

In the preceding section we showed that a simple covariance adjustment for the percentage of students taking the SAT is inappropriate on theoretical grounds (because as a posttreatment concomitant variable it adds bias). It can be dismissed on practical grounds as well because it is not sufficiently accurate to be useful in tracking state trends, nor in making state-by-state comparisons. To what extent does this same conclusion apply to the use of more complex adjustments for the purposes of drawing inferences from natural experiments utilizing states as the experimental units? It would seem that subsequent adjustments, such as those made by Powell and Steelman (1984) for other demographic variables (race, sex, and income), cannot overcome the shortcomings of the self-selection problem. This seems obvious. However, even if the first adjustment had worked, the same conclusion might still be valid. But we would not know this because we have no approximate validation group (analogous to the ACT–SAT concatenated group) on which to test the accuracy of the adjustment. Again the lesson is that one must do it right at sometime. In this instance, perhaps a cleverly sampled survey of individuals would allow the testing of the adjustment scheme and the estimation of its accuracy.

An example of current interest that exemplifies this problem is the attempt to draw a causal inference from data that relate the number of high school mathematics courses taken to the SAT mathematics score. This

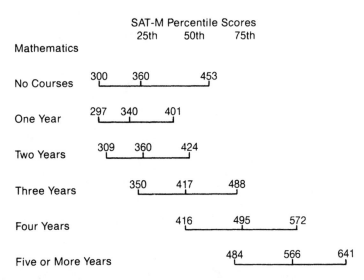

Figure 9. Relationship between the number of high school mathematics courses taken and the SAT mathematics scores.

result, shown in Figure 9 (from Ramist and Arbeiter, 1984) for all students who take the SAT, also holds in all subgroups so far examined (within sex and within ethnic group). The conclusions that appear in newspapers about these data is that the recent gains in SAT mathematics scores are caused by students taking more math courses in high school. Support for this conclusion comes from data such as that shown in Figure 9.

On the surface this seems like a compelling argument, yet a deeper look clouds the clarity of this conclusion. We see (Figure 10) that the more math courses, the higher the verbal score. Conceivably, taking more mathematics would help one's verbal ability, but a more plausible conclusion is that the verbal gains are probably reflecting the self-selection factor. Leaning heavily on the equated nature of the tests, one might say that the 121 point gain in median verbal score from those who take one year of mathematics to those who take five or more years reflects the self-selection of the more able students to a more rigorous academic program in high school. Thus, the 226 point gain in the SAT mathematics score might have a 121 point component of self-selection and a 105 point component of the effects of instruction. This seems plausible, and finds further support (Figure 11) when we note that there is a 124 point gain in the SAT mathematics score for those who take five or more years of a foreign language. Once again, we see the same estimate of self-selection.

These results are encouraging and seductive. All bets are off, however, after we see that more biology courses relate to *lower* SAT scores (Figure

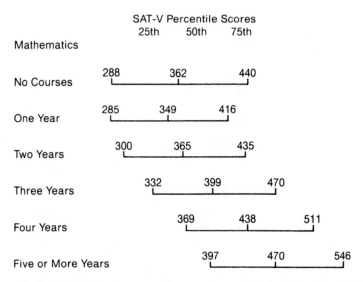

Figure 10. Relationship between the number of high school mathematics courses taken and the SAT verbal scores.

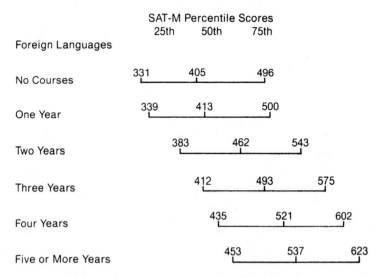

Figure 11. Relationship between the number of high school foreign language courses taken and the SAT mathematics scores.

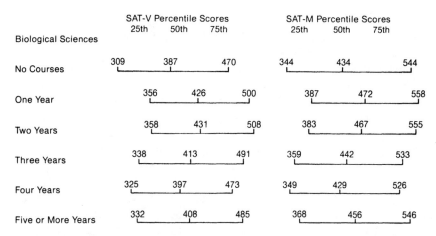

Figure 12. Relationship between the number of high school biology courses taken and the SAT verbal and mathematics scores.

12)! Something strange is happening. A variety of possible explanations for this outcome suggest themselves, but one thing is certain. No simple causal statements are likely to be correct. Is any simple statistical adjustment likely to clarify matters? The best chance to find out the right answer is to do the study right, without the artifact of self-selection. Since in this instance self-selection refers to students deciding how many courses to take, the proper experiment is probably impossible to do (random assignment to number of courses), but perhaps a more heroic data gathering effort, which would involve obtaining longitudinal data on the students as they progress through their course work, would provide the clues required. Alternatively, perhaps independent estimates of student ability would work. What we have is not sufficient for the inferences that are being drawn—that much at least is clear.

IV. But What Can We Do?

The examples shown were meant to point out that although the SAT can be a seductive candidate in the search for reliable educational indicators, it is a dangerous choice. This danger seems principally due to the unknown character of the self-selection process by which candidates decide to take the SAT. The simple adjustments that have so far been tried seem to work, but not well enough for the needs at hand. More is required.

It seems to me that the magic of statistical adjustment is an important and useful tool. We are not advocating its abandonment. Rather, we feel that direct assessment is a better choice when this is both practical and possible. Often it is not. For these situations it appears that an amalgam of direct assessment and statistical adjustment is called for. We might, for example, utilize survey methodology to obtain performance estimates in carefully selected subpopulations. We could then develop and test various adjustment models.

An SAT survey has much to recommend it, but it is still flawed. Is the motivation of its participants likely to be the same as under true testing situations? What are the costs likely to be?

An attractive alternative might be to attempt a concatenation of some of the in-place large-scale tests. The Armed Services Vocational Aptitude Battery (ASVAB) is given annually to more than a million high school seniors. The union of this population with those of the SAT and ACT could provide a still more accurate picture. Of course, to accomplish this we might need to modify the three tests a bit to allow their accurate equating. With luck this will only require adding some common items and then utilizing those tests that are plausibly equatable. This seems like a technically and politically difficult task, but not an impossible one.

An extremely attractive alternative is the expansion of the National Assessment of Educational Progress (NAEP). This survey is in operation now and has been for more than 15 years. It too has some shortcomings, for it does not allow state estimates, yet it is based upon a well-designed sample. An expansion of this to yield small area estimates would go a long way toward fulfilling the needs that SAT adjustments have attempted.

Of course, the strategy of coordinating NAEP with the other large-scale tests could yield huge benefits for a modest cost. Again, the first task would be the inclusion of enough common items to allow equating. Coordination seems to be the key element underlying all of these schemes.

While a vast interconnected array of coordinated tests might be a theoretical godsend, it could become an administrative horror. It would also strengthen the public misperception of the monolithic nature of the national testing enterprise. It also is not completely necessary. I view such an enterprise as being somewhat akin to the decennial census—it is important to do once in a while to correct adjustment models and for specific small area estimates, but not for day-to-day figures. For these we might be able to rely on *correctly* adjusted sample estimates, even from convenience samples. Such corrections are imperative if policy decisions are to be based upon differences in educational performance and not on variations in educational accounting.

Acknowledgments. This work was partially supported by a grant (#SES-8505591) from the National Science Foundation to the Educational Testing Service. Also my thanks to Bill Angoff for his careful reading and editorial suggestions.

Bibliography

Astin, A. (1971). *Predicting Academic Performance in College*. New York: Free Press.

Chase, C. and Barritt, L. (1966), "A table of concordance between ACT and SAT." *J. College Student Pers.*, 8, 105–108.

Cochran, W.G. (1957). "Analysis of covariance: Its nature and uses." *Biometrics*, 13, 261–281.

Page, E.B. and Feifs, H. (1985). "SAT scores and American states: Seeking for useful meaning." *J. Ed. Meas.*, 22, 305–312.

Powell, B. and Steelman, L.C. (1984). "Variations in state SAT performance: Meaningful or misleading?" *Harvard Ed. Rev.*, 54, 389–412.

Pugh, R. and Sassenrath, J. (1968). "Comparable scores for the CEEB Scholastic Aptitude Test and the American College Test program." *Meas. Eval. Guid.*, 1, 103–109.

Ramist, L. and Arbeiter, S. (1984). *Profiles, College-bound Seniors, 1983*. New York: The College Board.

Rosenbaum, P.R. (1984). "The consequences of adjustment for a concomitant variable that has been effected by the treatment." *J. Roy. Statist. Soc. Ser. A*, 147, 656–666.

Wainer, H., Holland, P.W., Swinton, S., and Wang, M. (1985). "On 'State Education Statistics'." *J. Ed. Statis.*, 10, 293–325.

Discussion 1:
The SAT As A
Social Indicator:
A Pretty Bad Idea

DISCUSSANT:
JOHN HARTIGAN

I'd like to congratulate Howard on an amusing and interesting talk and especially on the quality of his graphics.

The use of SAT scores to make comparisons in educational progress over time or between states is made difficult by different selectivity in different states at different times. As a result, a trend in scores may occur because more or fewer lower ability students take the test.

I think I can propose at least two ways of using the scores which would permit plausible comparisons between states and times. For example, in the states in which the ACT replaces the SAT, ACT scores may be converted to SAT scores. In the states where the SAT is used, we must determine the probability that a student of certain ability will take the test. It is reasonable to assume that, at the higher levels of ability (the highest, say, 5 or 10% of high school seniors), almost all students take the SAT. One may examine and track the highest 10% of SAT scores from one year to the next without selectivity problems, and that tracking would provide valid comparisons over time and between states. This does not include a sophisticated statistical method for estimating the probability that a student will take the test. In fact, a sound estimate would have to be a function of ability *and* income and race and perhaps other measures. This would require a model in which the probability of a student taking the SAT would depend upon various demographic factors and ability. Using such a model, one could obtain estimates and adjust the test scores for appropriate factors. This method will simply adjust for the selectivity factor, and, as there are large differences between individual states in educational progress, one would hope that the adjustments would reveal large differences. The fact that the adjustments were 50 or 60 points off the regression line should not be of concern—one would expect states to be different and to change over time.

Well, I think I've said my piece. It's always rather formidable to be followed by John Tukey in a discussion like this, but let John Tukey speak.

DISCUSSANT:
JOHN W. TUKEY

One of the advantages of having John Hartigan start is that one has less to say.

I came in knowing only the title of this talk, and thus I was reminded of the story of there being two kinds of lawyers; there are the lawyers who tell you that you *can't* do it and there are the lawyers who tell you *how* you can do it. I feared that Howard was going to come in the wrong one of the corresponding categories of statisticians. As far as I can see, he came in about half way in between.

I'm not sure whether I'm as optimistic as John Hartigan is about looking at the upper 5 and 10% of ability levels. I don't know enough about the facts to know whether this is going to be all that stable. It seems to me that the state-to-state variation from this sort of analysis is going to be, in part, like the security blanket of the comic strip character who only feels happy when he has it over his shoulder. "We knew Mississippi was at the bottom anyway, etc., etc. If these things don't come out right, we'll adjust it until they do. We haven't learned that much more, but maybe we've put another nail in the coffin of the people who didn't believe such things."

The year-to-year variation it seems to me deserves some more direct attention. I don't know whether Iowa is the only state that has a long-term effective state testing program, but I think an interesting calibration would be to calibrate the SAT results against the Iowa state results (and against state results for any other states with perhaps 10 or 15 years or more of reasonably comparable, reasonably universal testing). It isn't going to be an easy task, but it might leave you understanding how much of the year-to-year changes are accounted for by things that don't involve selection. If you could make this separation, you would be in a more peaceful situation.

HENRY BRAUN: Thank you John. Howard, would you like to take this opportunity to respond?

HOWARD WAINER: On the first point, I was reassured when Professor Tukey wasn't as sanguine as you (John Hartigan) are about the top 5 or 10% being useful.

JOHN HARTIGAN: He doesn't know how sanguine I am.

HOWARD WAINER: We tried out the notion of studying those high enough on the SAT so that one might consider, as plausible, the hypothesis that everyone who is at that high level took the test. We tried it for those individuals whose SAT scores were at 600 level or beyond. In round numbers that represents those that are one and a half standard deviations above the mean. As it turns out these are very small percentages. When considered as the percentage of all 18 year olds, this percentage gets smaller still. Additionally, the variation among states in the proportion of 18 year olds who are in that category is so small as to not be very useful. Specifically, the variation among the states on "proportion of 18 year olds over 600 on SAT verbal" ranged from 1.7 to 1.8%. Of course, trying to make inferences about the body of distribution from the extreme tail is too hazardous for sensible people.

The conclusion we drew is that if we choose 600 as the cut-off point, the percentages are too small. But if we lower that cut-off point, the plausibility of the selection hypothesis drops. Thus, the underlying assumption becomes increasingly implausible as the size of the measured population seems to become more useful.

Secondly, what I was trying to do in the concatenation of the SAT and ACT scores was to provide what the score for a state would have been had everyone taken it. That is presumably the same number that those who do covariance adjustments of the SAT scores were trying to estimate; specifically, those who adjust by "percentage taking SAT." I was hoping that those two numbers would be about the same or at least co-linear. When they weren't I took this as confirmation that the two procedures are not estimating the same thing.

JOHN HARTIGAN: What I'm saying is that this ignores all differences between the states. Why shouldn't one state, after adjustments, have quite a different true SAT score from another?

HOWARD WAINER: If both estimation methods are working, a state should have the same true SAT score using either scheme.

JOHN HARTIGAN: I don't agree with that.

DON RUBIN: One of the methods is an equating method, which tries to preserve the marginal distribution. The other is a regression prediction method, which has regression toward the mean, and so the predicted values will have less variance than the marginal distribution of the predicted scores. Thus, you wouldn't expect the two distributions to align.

HOWARD WAINER: I agree; I believe that the equating approach is a more reasonable one, but I was curious to know the extent to which the commonly used covariance adjustment method would get the same answer. Despite the problems with this latter procedure, I expected more alignment than I got.

DON RUBIN: I don't know how to judge that, unless you told me what the correlations were between the variables that you were adjusting for and the SAT. I'm just not sure whether the alignment is better or worse than I would have expected.

MEMBER OF AUDIENCE: To follow up on the point about the top "any percentage," even if you could say that you could accurately compare the top percentage across states and across time, most people would want to then extrapolate to the average of the whole state. You would still have the problem, in a slightly different form, of taking the top percentage and figuring out what is the distribution of the whole state.

JOHN HARTIGAN: That's true, but of course by doing it this way, you've made it explicit what you're doing. The trouble with the SAT scores is that people know that there is a varying selectivity and tend to just ignore the complexities. They say "The SAT score represents the students in the state." If you came out and said "Here are the scores of the top 15% of the state," it would be much less liable to misinterpretation. If the top 15% are doing something, there's only a small selection problem in there. Now it's true that small tails can be drifting off in any and all directions. Yet, if someone told me what was happening in the top 15% of the students in all the states, I would regard that as having surface validity, as they say.

HENRY BRAUN: If I could interject a comment, it seems to me that we're getting into a discussion of how you would use those results. You need to get a clear statement of what you wanted to do or, more specifically, what the policy maker wanted to do before you could decide whether or not John's suggestion of using the top 15% would be responsive to that aim. I can see a situation such as this: Suppose you could do a complete adjustment and get a very accurate assessment of how Mississippi and Delaware, say, compared on the SAT if everybody had taken it. You can imagine that Mississippi could argue, "Well, we have a different racial and ethnic composition. We should really look at how Mississippi would perform if it looked like Delaware." But what policy question would that answer? So, the analysis should be driven by policy considerations.

HOWARD WAINER: John, your idea is important in other ways. By being explicit about "the top 15%," you would then avoid the kinds of inferences you read about in the paper, such as how "compensatory educational programs are working because the minority scores have gone up 2 points this year." Perhaps this would not occur if one was explicit about stating that this was not being measured.

COMMENT FROM THE FLOOR: There's a small technical issue here about how you can find the top 15% or whatever percent. Howard was talking about cutting off at a particular score. John, it sounds like you're cutting off at a particular percentile in the scores. The problem with that is where the cut-off falls depends on how many people there are in the lower group. You have to cut off with some covariate like class rank, perhaps. Not the actual scores themselves.

JOHN HARTIGAN: I agree that that's a problem you have to worry about: where you do the cut-off. The simplest way to do the cut-off is to do it all on V + M. Then what you report is the percentage of high school students in that state (which is a known figure) who are between 600 and 610, 610 and 615, and so on. Like Howard was saying, you would come out with a report saying Mississippi has 0.1% above 1200 and Iowa has 12%. There'd be very big differences between the states in the percentages in the various high groups. I think you can control it both ways. You cut by SAT score and then you report actual percentages of high school students. I know there's another question here and that is "What is a valid high school student?" If you have the right policy you can make sure that all of your high school seniors are high scorers. You just don't promote anyone to be a high school senior who can't get a good score on the SAT.

DON RUBIN: I think there's something missing from this whole conversation, especially from a group of statisticians. I'm referring to the focus on point estimation for policy purposes without any statement of uncertainty assessment. One of the things statisticians are supposed to do, at least those who don't report baseball scores or give the number of people that fell in the mud at the end of a football game, is to give, along with a point estimate, a measure of uncertainty. In a very difficult problem like this, we try to provide an estimate adjusted for some selection bias, but an important component of the answer is to give an honest measure of the uncertainty of the estimate. I know the push is always to give a point estimate, because that's what the policy maker needs. But nevertheless, the scientific thing to do is to not just focus on the point estimate, but to say how bad the answer is. I've heard nothing about that today, except indirectly in John's suggestion about trying to estimate a quantity for which the point estimate may be so good that the uncertainty assessment is unimportant. I think that's what he's driving toward. I suspect that the uncertainty associated with the mean of the whole unselected population is certainly very great. But there's still a chance of being able to nail it down under some models, and I think that displaying the dependence on models is an important issue.

HENRY BRAUN: I think that one of Howard's plots—the plot of the Powell and Steelman adjusted residuals against the concatenation of the ACT and the SAT—is trying to get a baseline and an estimate. It then says that because there is so much uncertainty there and so much variation, that we should be fairly uncertain about those point estimates.

DON RUBIN: I would regard that as saying that they're both failures in some sense. They were trying to estimate different things. I'm not sure how to regard that, but I think a more appropriate approach would be to try to develop some measure of how much the answer can change under a range of plausible models.

HENRY BRAUN: That might be truly depressing.

DON RUBIN: That may be truly depressing, but that also may be truly honest.

JOHN TUKEY: If you're really going to assess uncertainty in a situation, what you must refrain from is assessing only the *overt statistical uncertainty*. You've got to try to assess the uncertainty of the biases—that means you have to put the necks of a certain number of statisticians and other experts on the line. It's peaceful to only estimate an internal standard deviation and stop. Really facing up to the biases is a thing we haven't practiced.

Self-Selection and Performance-Based Ratings: A Case Study in Program Evaluation

BURTON SINGER

I. Introduction

Randomized clinical trials are widely regarded as the method of choice for evaluating the efficacy of therapeutic treatments in medicine. For a critique of this attitude and a balanced discussion of alternative strategies, the reader should consult Feinstein (1985). Despite the rigorous nature of randomized trials, their domain of applicability is essentially restricted to studies where the investigator can control the structure of the population to be investigated and where the number of conditions (or circumstances) involved in comparisons is small in number. Programs in which voluntary self-selection for entry is an essential feature and in which the full treatment involves not only drug therapy but a variety of counseling services and an appropriate administrate structure do not lend themselves to evaluation by conventional randomized trials. In fact, the act of randomization into a program could destroy one of the central processes under investigation; namely, the process of voluntary self-selection.

For the evaluation of complex programs with self-selection of entrants, one is frequently forced to settle for a less rigorous methodology then controlled randomized trials.

The purpose of this paper is to exhibit a strategy and an underlying rationale for the evaluation of complex programs for which:

(i) voluntary self-selection into a treatment program is a condition of entry;

(ii) it is unknown whether the decision criteria for entry used by volunteers are the same or different from those of nonvolunteers;

(iii) the program has a multiplicity of components constituting the treatment; and

(iv) a control group from the target population cannot be assembled.

Conditions (i)–(iv) are the context for evaluation of Methadone Maintenance Treatment (MMT) programs for rehabilitation of chronic heroin addicts; these particular programs are the focus of the present paper. The methodological principles underlying the evaluation of MMT programs are applicable in a wide variety of settings which lie outside the domain of randomized trials and include the evaluation of manpower training programs, family planning programs in developing countries, and rehabilitation programs for chronic alcoholics. An interesting aspect of MMT program evaluation is that control groups of chronic addicts who are not volunteers for treatment cannot be assembled for comparison purposes. In fact, the act of assembling such a group—aside from the practical difficulties of doing it—would interfere with one of the natural processes in the investigation; namely, the opportunity for voluntary entry into a program at some time after the follow-up is initiated. Thus, comparing the behavior of patients in an MMT program with some kind of standard reduces to a comparison with a natural history of heroin addiction developed from multiple studies, none of which is the specific MMT program evaluation itself. Furthermore, comparison of MMT clinics with one another is an indirect process involving the comparison of each clinic with historical controls (i.e., earlier clinics) and other contemporary clinics via a series of performance indices. This leads to the strategy of performance-based ratings for MMT program evaluation in particular and complex programs with self-selection of entrants in general.

In Section II we review instances of the heroin abuse and treatment situation in Hong Kong, Sweden, and New York. This serves to clarify the scope of the heroin addiction problem and briefly indicates some of the variety of interventions which have been put forth with the aim of controlling the addiction problem.

In Section III we describe the natural history of heroin addiction and view this as the baseline for comparison of voluntary MMT program participants with what would have happened to them if they had continued their daily self-administration of heroin. Section IV contains examples of a variety of intervention strategies aimed at controlling addiction. One of the interventions is a natural experiment which provided the best evidence to date that an addicted population could voluntarily give up daily heroin use and abstain from further heroin abuse without any medication or formal treatment program.

In Section V we present a rationale for evaluation of MMT programs via performance-based rating indices. This is tantamount to a comparison of each clinic with both historical controls and other contemporary clinics and represents what we regard as the maximum level of rigor currently attainable for comparative evaluation of entire MMT programs. Such an evaluation strategy stands in sharp contrast to the randomized trials of methadone versus placebo where the primary purpose of the trials was to evaluate voluntary retention in a given program for prior chronic heroin abusers.

We conclude, in Section VI, with a discussion of the domain of program evaluation via performance-based ratings and present statements of problems for future research.

II. Heroin Addiction and Interventions

Heroin abuse occurs in widely disparate environments and on a diversity of scales. Nevertheless, the natural history of heroin addiction seems to be invariant no matter what the geographic setting. As a prelude to developing a characterization of this natural history and to provide a context for a consideration of treatment programs and their evaluation, we review the addiction situation in three qualitatively different settings.

(1) On the basis of a 1979 case-finding survey (see Olsson et al., 1981), it was estimated that Sweden, with a population of roughly 8 million people, had between 3000 and 4000 intravenous abusers of heroin and that approximately one-half of these were heroin addicts with compulsive drug-seeking behavior. The only natural treatment program is MMT, established in 1967 and modeled on the initial American programs introduced by Dole and Nyswander (1965). Although the catchment area has been all of Sweden, there have been only 170 admissions between 1967 and 1979 (Gunne and Gronbladh, 1981; Gunne, 1983). Acceptance criteria into MMT programs remained constant throughout this time period and were the following:

(a) at least 20 years old and a minimum of 4 years history of compulsive intravenous misuse of opiates as documented by hospital records;
(b) withdrawal symptoms and urinary opioid excretion;
(c) a minimum of three earlier completed detoxifications; and
(d) not arrested, not serving sentence, and no dominating abuse of non-opiate drugs.

The effect and concentration of methadone in MMT patients stabilized on an adequate daily dose (usually from 50 to 100 mg) is illustrated in Figure 1. The concentration of methadone in the blood is kept at all times

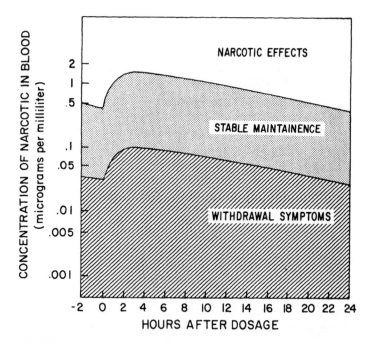

Figure 1. Effect and concentration of methadone for methadone-maintained patients. From Dole (1980).

above the threshold for withdrawal symptoms. The peak concentration in a stabilized patient remains well below the threshold for narcotic effects. When an MMT patient is stabilized on a correct daily dose of methadone, he is functionally normal, protected from narcotic effects by his pharmacological tolerance of the drug *and* from withdrawal symptoms by the constant presence of methadone in his bloodstream.

(2) Using data from the Hong Kong Central Registry of Drug Abuse in 1981 (see Action Committee Against Narcotics, 1981), it was estimated that there were approximately 40,000 drug addicts, 85% of whom abused heroin at the time of the first report. This addict population comes from the more than 5 million persons (living in an environment where population density is 25,400/km^2) who make up the population of Hong Kong. The 1981 addict prevalence stands in sharp contrast to the estimated 150,000 to 200,000 addicts found in a 1959 opinion survey that was based on informal policy assessments, which could be subject to very substantial error.

A major source of decline in the addict population can be attributed to mass government sponsored advertising on billboards, radio, television, and school programs combined with increasingly intense law enactment and enforcement against drug sellers (see Newman, 1984). Furthermore, in 1975 the Hong Kong government decided to *ensure* treatment to *all* addicts willing to accept it. The addict population in 1975 was estimated to number 50,000 persons. MMT was the only program that could be expanded rapidly enough and sustained on a sufficiently large scale to accomplish this goal. There was also explicit government resolve to continue to support drug-free therapeutic programs as well. The Hong Kong effort, with support from the highest levels of government, is unmatched anywhere else in the world.

(3) In 1972 a *lower bound* on the number of heroin addicts in New York City was estimated to be 250,000 persons (Dole, 1972a) out of a population of roughly 8 million. MMT was initiated in 1964 at the Rockefeller University Hospital in New York (Dole and Nyswander, 1965; Dole et al., 1966), treating only a pilot population of 10–50 patients. By 1971 the caseload in New York for MMT had evolved to 25,000 addicts entering treatment, but with roughly 20% of these discharged for persistent and disruptive antisocial behavior. This suggested that additional techniques for control of psychopathic behavior and for treatment of nonnarcotic abuses be developed as a routine part of the overall MMT program. This has subsequently been incorporated as a central aspect of MMT programs. Although there has been considerable long-term success (meaning rehabilitation of former heroin addicts) with the early entrants into MMT (Dole and Joseph, 1979), with expansion of programs various size-related rigidities have limited their success.

III. Natural History of Heroin Addiction

The incidence of heroin abuse varies dramatically with geographical location and time-period-specific macrolevel events such as the end of World War II, major recessions, and the Vietnam War protest movement. In urban ghetto neighborhoods it is frequently associated with grossly inadequate parental support in early childhood, unemployment in the teen and young adult years, and strong peer influence supporting heroin usage. Once heroin abuse has begun, most such persons go through periods of temporary abstinence, but after six to eight years of heroin use they usually persist as chronic, daily drug-seeking users. With increasing age the death rate among these chronic users rises rapidly and is substantially larger than the age-specific mortality rates for nonheroin users (Vaillant, 1966b).

Persons abusing heroin for less than one year, or at most two years, who started in the age range of 16–22 years (even if they are daily users for spells of several months or even one year) tend to revert to permanent abstinence with no treatment. Abstinence facilitates employment, which in turn is a critical condition for rehabilitation.

Persons continuing sustained, virtually daily, heroin abuse for more than three years either voluntarily enter MMT, a drug-free therapeutic program, or a center where withdrawal is the physical treatment supplemented by psychological counseling and job search assistance, or they die with a frequency that increases dramatically with the number of years of daily usage. It is suspected (see Dole and Nyswander, 1968) that this relatively small subset of the ever-using population has suffered a heroin-related metabolic change that makes it virtually impossible for them to simply revert voluntarily to temporary abstinence. For them maintenance on methadone should be viewed (but rarely is by regulatory bodies) as analogous to insulin maintenance of diabetics. Among chronic (more than three years) heroin addicts an increasing fraction are institutionalized with increasing years of usage, largely to prevent the frequent robberies that are necessary to sustain the high cost of two to five heroin injections per day. The institutionalized population either goes through withdrawal in prison or is treated with methadone (see, e.g., Dole, 1972b), but upon release these people almost invariably relapse to regular daily use.

A more focused longitudinal picture of the natural history of heroin addiction can be obtained from studies of Vaillant (1966a, b, c, d, 1973) on a U.S. Public Health Service Hospital population in Lexington, Kentucky. The study group consisted of 50 male narcotic addicts from New York City who averaged 3.5 years of active addiction and were admitted to the hospital in Lexington between August 1, 1952, and January 31, 1953. Prior to admission, 49 of the 50 addicts had been using opiates several times each day. Figure 2 gives an overview of the natural history of addiction of this

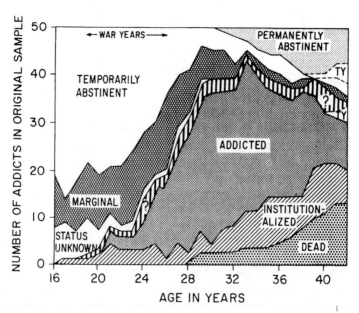

Figure 2. Relationship of drug use to age. From Vaillant (1966b).

group. This graph attempts to reflect the probability of active addition at any given age. However, it is important to recognize that individual addiction histories involve transitions back and forth between periods of active addiction and temporary abstinence.

For every calendar year after the age of 16, each addict was classified as abstinent, addicted, or possibly addicted depending on what his status had been for most of that year. Addicts abstinent for at least three years and without known subsequent relapse were classed as "permanently abstinent." The category "institutionalized" was used if the addict had been in a prison or hospital for more than 11 months of the calendar year; "marginal" was used if the addict was either using drugs intermittently or had engaged in criminal pursuits.

Many more addicts achieved temporary abstinence than sustained it. However, roughly 40% seem to have achieved stable abstinence by 42 years of age. Although at age 40 less than 25% of the population remained addicted, this also is a reflection of the fact that two out of five persons were either dead or had been institutionalized for prolonged periods of time.

Of those addicts who became permanently abstinent, two-thirds found stable employment; supported themselves and a family; did not engage in

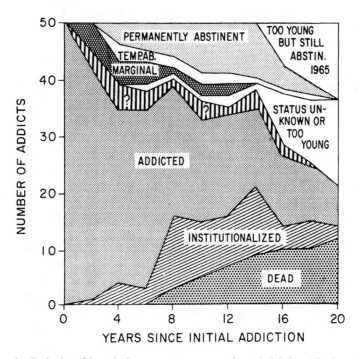

Figure 3. Relationship of drug use to years since initial addiction. From Vaillant (1966b).

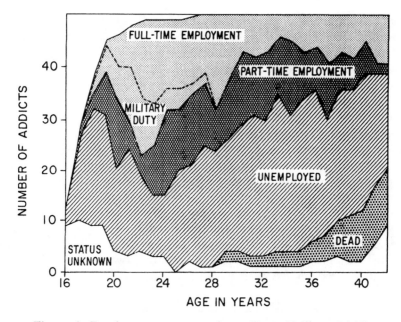

Figure 4. Employment status and age. From Vaillant (1966b).

serious alcohol, barbiturate, or tranquilizer abuse; and refrained from further criminal activity. In essence, this indicates that the chronically delinquent urban addict can and frequently does learn to live successfully without drugs.

Figure 3 gives an alternative perspective on the same population. For each year following initial addiction, roughly 2% of addicts became permanently abstinent and 1% died or became chronically institutionalized. In the course of an addiction "career," the average addict spent only six years actively addicted. Roughly five more years were spent in jail and one year in a hospital. The average addict was known to have been withdrawn from drugs either in jail or in the hospital a total of nine times and, thus, relapsed a minimum of eight times.

From the vantage point of social disability, Figure 4 indicates the extent of unemployment in addict populations. In particular out of the 25 year period of the study, the average addict was neither in jail or actually addicted for 13 of these years. Nevertheless, he was abstinent and fully employed for less than 4 years out of the 25. This characterization of the natural history of heroin addiction forms the baseline against which treatment programs are to be evaluated. Clearly permanent abstinence and sustained full-time employment are primary goals of any treatment program.

The patterns of heroin use described above are a useful starting point for an unstanding of addiction as a developmental process; however, the fundamental question of *why* human addicts dose themselves remains unanswered. Alternative theories of heroin addiction in which this is largely viewed as a metabolic disease compete with psychological theories which claim that basic character defects and sociopathic behavior are generic to the potential addict and are associated with so-called addictive personalities. Definitive evidence in either direction or support for a clearly delineated combination of psychological and metabolic defects still remains to be developed. For a concise and informative review of theories of heroin addiction, see Dole and Nyswander (1968).

IV. Varieties of Interventions

A. Hong Kong

Shortly after the 1975 massive prevention, education, and treatment campaign was initiated in Hong Kong, a network of 20 MMT clinics was in place serving 8000 patients per day, patients who otherwise would have continued using heroin or opium purchased from the illicit market. Within 5 years after this program was initiated, the number of addicts sent to prison declined by almost 75%. Strong evidence that MMT played a major role in this decline comes from a controlled randomized trial of methadone versus placebo (Newman and Whitehill, 1979). Retention rates in programs were a major outcome of interest.

In the Hong Kong randomized trial (Figure 5), the sample was obtained by taking 100 consecutive addicts who voluntarily applied for treatment in the clinic. The admission criteria were the following:

(a) male, aged 22 to 58 years, with a documented history of heroin addiction of at least 4 years duration and at least one previous addiction treatment episode;
(b) evidence of current addiction to heroin as determined by three consecutive positive urine tests for morphine;
(c) a resident with proven fixed address in Kowloon in a district in the vicinity of the clinic; and
(d) absence of major psychiatric or medical illness, including tuberculosis, peptic ulcer, or history of psychosis.

The 100 volunteers were pair matched by age, addiction history, criminal record, and family status to yield 50 similar pairs. One member of each pair was assigned randomly to methadone and the other to a placebo treatment, the assignment being known only to the pharmacist who prepared the medications.

All subjects were stabilized initially on methadone (60 mg/day) for a two-week period. Then the medication was withdrawn from the control

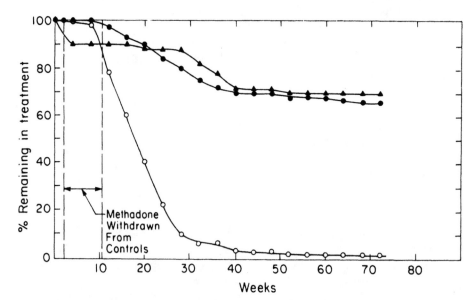

- ● Received Methadone
- ○ Controls (Methadone Withdrawn Between Weeks 2–10)
- ▲ Dropouts from Control Group, Retreated with Methadone
  (Hong Kong Discharged Prisoner's Aid Society, 1972–1974)

Figure 5. Retention rates in Hong Kong randomized double blind trial of methadone versus placebo. From Dole and Singer (1979).

group at a rate of 1 mg/day until they reached zero dose. Thereafter the control subjects received only a flavored placebo which was said to be indistinguishable in taste from methadone. The retention rates in the two groups were markedly different, as indicated in Figure 5.

After 9 months 75% of the methadone patients remained in the treatment, while the control group had declined to less than 10% of its original size. By the end of the 72-week study, only one person (2%) remained in the control group, while 62% (31 of 50) were continuing with methadone. Moreover, when the dropouts from the control group were retreated, this time with methadone, their retention rate and rehabilitation were the same as had been observed in the original methadone group. The employment rate for patients accepting methadone averaged about 80%; the subjects in the control group dropped out too fast for this or other social indices to be significant. Two-thirds of the group receiving methadone were scored by staff workers (who were blind to the medication being received) as improved in the categories of financial support to family, concern toward family, behavior at home, communication with family members, and acceptance by family. When the control group was retreated with methadone, their employment rate increased to 80% and other measures of social rehabilitation became comparable to those of the original methadone group. The average maintenance dose of methadone in the trial was 80 mg/day.

An important feature of this study that supports the ability to generalize conclusions about retention rates is that for those subjects receiving methadone, the rates are almost identical to those in programs in New York City (Newman, 1976, 1977) which adhere to the policies and procedures originally proposed by Dole and Nyswander (1968) but for which no randomized trials were conducted. This similarity of retention rates is particularly striking in view of the obvious, marked differences in the social, economic, and political environments in which drugs are used, as well as the differences in the manner of heroin use and the characteristics of addicts in Hong Kong and in New York.

B. Early New York Methadone Clinics

During the first two years of operation of New York City methadone clinics, good medical and counseling services were provided for a small research group (10–50 patients). In 1965–1967 a total of roughly 660 patients had entered either research or pilot MMT programs. Admission criteria were (a) a minimum of four years of heroin addiction; (b) age range from 20 to 40; and (c) no evidence of major medical conditions, alcohol abuse, or polydrug abuse. After ten years, 60% of this cohort was still in treatment, some having left MMT programs and returned one or more times. A subset of this group, comprising 39% of the original cohort, had remained continuously in treatment for ten or more years (Dole and Joseph, 1979). Approximately half of these subjects had shown a rapid improvement, becoming socially productive and free from drug abuse within the first two years. For almost all of this favorable subgroup, their clinic records showed no problem from the day of admission. Relief of heroin hunger apparently was sufficient to permit their social rehabilitation. Another one-fourth had responded more slowly, reaching socially acceptable status only after four years or more of treatment. The remaining one-fourth had declined in function in the last five years, in some cases after an initially favorable response to treatment. In most cases the problem causing the decline in this group was alcoholism. None of the 242 long-term maintenance patients had returned to daily use of illicit opiates.

Although the performance of the "continuously-in-treatment" group indicates the potential high efficacy of MMT programs, it is important to also assess the program by considering the response of discharged and dropout subjects to retreatment among those who volunteered for retreatment. The experience in the initial 1966–1967 cohort was that where treatment was stopped, the majority relapsed. During additional cycles of treatment (each time involving only a fraction of those discharged), there were dramatic reductions in opiate abuse during treatment but mostly followed by relapse after detoxification and subsequent discharge. Thus, MMT is effective in reducing the use of illicit opiates while the medication is being taken, but relapse is likely to occur when treatment is stopped. MMT controls, but does not cure, narcotics addiction.

C. Vietnam Veterans

Robins et al. (1975) studied a random sample of 963 U.S. Army enlistees leaving Vietnam in September 1971. Of these, 470 represented a general sample of all enlistees returning at that time and 495 represented a drug-positive sample whose urine had been positive for opiates at the time of departure.

Before arrival in Vietnam, hard drug use was largely casual and only 1% had ever been addicted to narcotics. In Vietnam almost 50% of the general sample tried narcotics and 20% reported opiate addiction. After return, to the United States, usage and addiction decreased to pre-Vietnam levels. It is important for our purposes to consider frequency and duration of use among men who tried narcotics in Vietnam. Table 1 (from Robins et al., 1975) gives a breakdown according to frequency and duration of usage.

A major conclusion of the Robins et al. (1975, p. 961) study is that: "Opiates are not so addictive that use is necessarily followed by addiction nor that once addicted, an individual is necessarily addicted permanently." This conclusion stands in sharp contrast to the relapse rates for MMT discharge patients, but a major factor here is the dramatic difference in duration of addiction. *All* early MMT patients would be in the more than weekly category in Table 1 *and* for at least four years. Whether MMT discharge patients would respond to a dramatic change in setting by

Table 1. Narcotics frequency and duration of use of U.S. troops in Vietnam[a]

Frequency and duration	Percentage of users
< 5 times	24
> 5, not more than weekly	9
More than weekly	
< 6 months	20
6–8 months	23
> 9 months	25

[a] From Robins et al. (1975)

voluntary abstinence, as did the Vietnam veterans, is simply not known. As mentioned previously, however, there is an indication that after three to four years of daily heroin usage, a metabolic change occurs in addicts which makes voluntary abstinence virtually impossible. Strong evidence supporting this suggestion awaits further studies in the future. Nevertheless, it would be of interest to find a population of three to four year daily users on whom a dramatic change in setting could be instituted, thereby providing a genuine direct comparison with the Vietnam veterans on voluntary abstinence.

D. Drug-free Therapeutic Communities

Early treatment programs for drug abuse, designed primarily to detoxify heroin addicts, were distinctly unsuccessful in their influence on subsequent behavior of the patients. Addicts detoxified and discharged to the community soon returned to drug use, often developing larger habits than they had before. The therapeutic community sought to develop the internal resources of addicts to deal with problems in living, in addition to detoxifying them. The first therapeutic community, after which virtually all others were modeled, was Synanon in Santa Monica, California. The attainment of drug-free status; the development of alternative, more effective life styles enabling members to cope with problems in living; and return to society are the major objectives of most communities. Synanon is an exception which does not share the objective of return or reentry. It views society as so corrupt that it is not worth reentering and has built its own structurally separate society that includes schools for children, work for adults, and facilities of all kinds for all ages.

Long-term follow up data comparable to that which has been collected on MMT programs (Dole and Joseph, 1979) are not available for evaluating drug-free therapeutic communities. Thus, what is sometimes regarded as a major alternative to MMT cannot be assessed in terms of its potential for rehabilitation of heroin addicts. There is, however, one evaluation of drug-free communities which is worthy of study for its methodological insights, despite the fact that it does not deal with heroin addiction. This is the volume by Brook and Whitehead (1980) focusing on amphetamine abuse—a very different problem from heroin addiction.

V. Program Evaluation

All treatment programs for heroin addiction have as goals the termination of heroin use and, secondarily, stable employment and family life. Any evaluation of such programs, however, must set a finite time horizon on the follow-up period and must, of necessity, be ad hoc in defining success in terms of a maximal observable duration of abstinence. So-called drug-free programs extend this goal to abstinence from *any* kind of illicit drugs. They also exclude the use of methadone even when used beneficially as a medication. A divergence of perceived goals—total abstinence versus just termination of heroin use—has led to much confusion about these programs and has not provided a basis for comparative evaluation.

The studies summarized in Section IV indicate that there should be a stratification of heroin users into at least three distinct groups for purposes of evaluating narcotics control programs. These are (1) early users for whom daily use does not exceed one year, (2) intermediate users for whom daily use persists between one and two years, and (3) chronic users who persist in daily use for more than two years. In the group of early users are persons who, given proper motivation and change of personal circumstance, will spontaneously abstain from heroin abuse. The chronic users are persons very unlikely to stop permanently, and they form the population eligible for voluntary MMT program participation. The Vietnam veterans study of Robins et al. (1975) provided the primary evidence for the potential of treatment-free recovery in the early user population. Finally, the intermediate users are a heterogeneous collection, some of whose members may be incapable of voluntary abstinence after only one year of daily heroin use, while others may have this capability even after two years of daily use.

Although it would be desirable to be able to extrapolate the conclusions from comparisons made in evaluating one or more treatment regimes to the general addict populations defined by the early, intermediate, and chronic classification, this is not possible because of the necessity of having entry to any program based on voluntary self-selection by the addict. What the response of a chronic addict who does not voluntarily enter an MMT program would be if he or she did enroll is anyone's guess. A decision to enroll is, in the mind of a chronic addict, the result of an interaction between his or her personal misery experienced during ongoing heroin abuse and the possibility of hope about rehabilitation which the existence of MMT presents. When hope dominates misery, an enrollment decision usually follows; however, there is no obvious way to assess how close a chronic addict who has never sought treatment is to the "continue misery" versus hope boundary. It seems plausible that those most likely to be rehabilitated are in fact the population of volunteers, i.e., those who have a strong sense of hope about rehabilitation. Indeed, the most successful MMT participants are criminals who, prior to program entry, focused on stealing to maintain a heroin habit. The key feature for rehabilitation of this criminal population is that as chronic heroin users they minimally deviate from their peer group of origin. In contrast to this situation, more educated middle class people undergo an enormous shift in peer group structure when initiating heroin use and then attempting rehabilitation. This seems to present major difficulties in their rehabilitation process. Thus, it seems plausible that a vision of hope is more readily generated in the criminal population and that they can somehow perceive the relatively short distance between their present situation and what would for them constitute rehabilitation. The essential point of this discussion for our purposes is that conclusions about narcotics treatment programs are all conditional on membership in the population of volunteers for entry. If MMT programs were not available, then, as implied by the natural history characterization, early death or prolonged institutionalization would be the likely outcome even for the chronic addict population "volunteers." We also stress that an effective prediction methodology which sharply distinguishes volunteers in the chronic addict population from nonvolunteers in this group is not available.

Evaluation of early New York MMT programs was subject to considerable criticism because randomized trials of methadone versus placebo were not carried out within the chronic addict volunteer population. From the point of view of evaluating the efficacy of methadone both as a narcotic blockade *and* for willingness of patients to voluntarily accept regular medically prescribed doses, the lack of controlled randomized trials might be viewed as having seriously jeopardized wide-scale acceptance of MMT programs by the federal government and even the medical community. However, the early informal anecdotal evidence indicated that a proper dosage schedule of methadone was a necessary but *insufficient* condition for successful treatment outcome—success in this case meaning sustained abstinence from heroin and at least part-time (if not full-time) employment and a stable family life.

In the original development of MMT programs (Dole and Nyswander, 1965), it became clear that effective counseling services, both psychological and in the form of assistance in acquiring jobs, were as important as a proper methadone dosage schedule. Sensitivity of clinic personnel to the special problems of chronic addicts and the importance of treating the patients with respect and understanding were central characteristics of successful programs. Also critical to clinic success was an administrative structure that was minimally intrusive to the patient. These characteristics indicate that a successful clinic is characterized by the *simultaneous* occurrence of positive performance on several dimensions by clinic personnel and proper administration of methadone. Thus, a randomized trial of programs would properly have had to vary not only the drug administration protocol but also counseling methods and administrative structure. This would lead to a complicated factorial design in which there was a high-order interaction (unknown *a priori*) that it would be necessary to detect to identify the successful program. The data requirements for such formal experimentation would have far exceeded the number of available clinics. Thus, a more informal trial-and-error process leading to the first few successful clinics (leaving the definition of success open-ended at first) was not only the procedure of choice for clinic development but also for performance evaluation.

The comparison of what is subsequently defined to be a successful program with earlier versions tried out in the development process can be viewed as an evaluation with historical controls. This seems to be the only feasible evaluation mechanism for MMT programs and leads naturally to the use of performance-based ratings. The impossibility of comparative evaluations using matched control clinics arises from the inherent variability in the voluntary input population and combinatorial constraints. Matching clinics on characteristics of personnel, administrative practices, and socioeconomic characteristics of the input population would require both an abundance of clinics and input population sizes which far exceed what is actually in existence. Furthermore, there is no way to ensure that the self-selecting input population to one clinic is a sufficiently close match to that of a comparison clinic so that detected differences could defensibly be attributed only to differences in details of the programs. This situation forces us to reconsider precisely what questions are answerable with historical controls and whether they can be viewed as providing an adequate performance evaluation.

It is useful to begin a consideration of answerable questions by again restating the goals of MMT programs. The central target is to stop the use of heroin and other illicit narcotics. The secondary goals are social rehabilitation and elimination of other forms of drug and alcohol abuse if present. Although the secondary goals are important, they are not likely to be achieved if the program fails to stop the use of heroin. Thus, we need to know whether chronic addicts stop heroin use over a substantial time period (at least one year) following entry to an MMT program and whether there is also evidence of social rehabilitation and reduction in abuse of nonnarcotic drugs and alcohol if this is also an issue. Given the experimental constraints described above, the basic evaluation strategy is to first identify MMT programs which had the best performance among those in the early programs of 1965–1967. Examination of retention rates and social rehabilitation records for these programs delineates what is *actually achievable* with chronic addict populations. This is then used as a baseline for comparison of the same and other clinics with previously achieved high standards.

Table 2 contains rating standards for MMT programs guided by the performance of New York State clinics. This "index of continuing problems" is a rating scale designed for comparisons between MMT clinics only. It is not intended for comparisons of MMT with other programs such as drug-free therapeutic communities. The index measures the persistence (or recurrence) of a problem that was present before admission. For the first two problems listed in Table 2—not in treatment and use of heroin—the pretreatment prevalence is 100%. Therefore, these two categories show the total dropout rate and the persistence of illicit use of narcotics among

Table 2. Rating the performance of programs according to residual behavioral and social problems after one year of treatment

Problem	Treatment available	Rating index[a] (%)			Factors associated with poor performance
		Good	Fair	Poor	
Dropped out within one year	Therapeutic relationships	< 20	20–40	> 40	Rigid rules; punitive attitudes
Use of heroin or other illicit narcotics while in treatment	Methadone	< 5	5–10	> 10	Inadequate dose
Alcoholism	Supportive services	< 90	90–110	> 110	No specific treatment available
Abuse of nonnarcotic drugs	Supportive services	< 40	40–60	> 60	No specific treatment available
Criminal activities	Supportive services	< 10	10–30	> 30	Continued association with criminals; unemployment
Unemployment	Supportive services	< 70	70–90	> 90	Depressed economy

[a] Index of continuing problems = $\dfrac{\text{prevalence one year after admission}}{\text{prevalence before admission}} \times 100$.

patients in treatment. Patients who have dropped out after less than one year of treatment are assumed to be readdicted in the absence of evidence to the contrary. For the other categories, the pretreatment prevalence of the problem varies with the population admitted for treatment. In all categories, the lower the rating index, the more successful the program has been in eliminating the problem (Dole et al., 1982).

Routine use of these performance-based ratings—with possible revision of the reference scores if special clinics achieve new low levels on the rating indices—provides a natural methodology for MMT program evaluation initially (i.e., for new programs) and for continued monitoring. The answerable questions in a clinic evaluation are of the form:

(1) Has this clinic achieved retention rates over a given follow-up period (e.g., one year) which are as high or higher than the best rates achieved in the baseline clinics?

(2) Are the criminal activity or unemployment rates as low or lower than those achieved in the best baseline clinics?

It is, of course, presumed that the top performances among the reference clinics were regarded as successes and that the addiction history of persons entering these clinics deviated sharply from the natural history of chronic addicts for whom early death and prolonged institutionalization were the most probable outcomes. An important characteristic of questions (1) and (2) is that they only focus on coarse features of clinics and the patient population. Indeed, it is only at this coarse level that meaningful program evaluation can be carried out, given the complexity of MMT programs and the voluntary self-selection of the patient population. More refined comparisons would either require unrealistically large numbers of clinics or strong modeling assumptions which, for the present, could not be easily defended.

VI. Discussion and Conclusions

When a treatment program is targeted at a well-defined population (e.g., addicts with more than two years of daily use of heroin), it is natural to want to extrapolate conclusions from the performance evaluation of a few clinics to clinics in general *and* to their impact on the full target population. However, when:

  (i) voluntary self-selection into a treatment program is a condition of entry;

  (ii) it is unknown whether the decision criteria for entry used by volunteers are the same or different from those of nonvolunteers;

  (iii) the program has a multiplicity of components constituting the treatment, such as methadone, psychological counseling services, and job search assistance; and

  (iv) a concurrent control group cannot be assembled,

then extrapolation of clinic evaluation results to clinics in general and generalization of conclusions about individual patients to the full target population are not justified.

In this setting, the questions which are answerable in any program evaluation tend to involve comparisons between a given clinic and the best current clinic performance or historically developed standards for the program as such. Individual responses for persons in treatment are evaluated by comparison with a characterization of the natural history of the phenomena under investigation that is developed from other data sources. Extrapolation of conclusions about individual responses to the target population are not defensible unless one is willing to invoke strong assumptions about the process of voluntary self-selection into treatment and about the behavioral differences between volunteers and nonvolunteers. For an extensive discussion of various modeling alternatives and their role in program evaluation where self-selection is a central ingredient, see Heckman and Robb (1986, this volume). It is our view that much sharper quantification via a series of empirical studies on addict populations would be necessary before analytical selection bias adjustments, as considered by Heckman and Robb, could defensibly be applied to chronic addict populations enrolling in MMT programs.

Selection bias adjustments not withstanding, the evaluation of complex programs via performance-based ratings seems to be a natural strategy in which the detailed nature of the heterogeneity of the potential treatment population and of the program administration itself are highly time varying. Clearly this situation is not unique to MMT programs, and virtually every issue we have raised about their evaluation has its counterpart in efforts to evaluate such diverse treatments as manpower training programs, new grade school educational innovations, family planning programs, and health care programs for the aged.

In comparison with the strategies discussed by Heckman and Robb (1986, this volume), the MMT evaluations discussed in this paper are relatively informal. They lead naturally to a research agenda which would provide a deeper understanding of the methodology used herein and a more detailed delineation of the general character of questions answerable in the environment described by points (i)–(iv) above versus questions answerable in randomized trials and observational studies with varying gradations of comparison groups. In this regard, see Feinstein (1985) for an extensive list of evaluation designs and examples of contexts in which they are relevant. The central research questions include the following:

(1) How should we assess uncertainty in a comparison of durations of heroin use for persons volunteering for MMT with mean duration of use from a natural history characterization based on multiple data sources?

(2) In the development of successful complex programs, can the existing multistage selection methods (see Finney, 1984, for a review) be adapted and exploited so that the highest achievable performance levels can be reached as early as possible after the initiation of the development process? This would, of course, require a coordinated program development process across a multiplicity of sites. It should also lead to rapid detection of the high-order interaction which, as in MMT programs, characterizes the conditions of successful operation.

(3) Would a hybrid strategy of multistage selection and randomized trials on portions of a program, such as the Hong Kong and Swedish methadone versus placebo trials, provide a more effective program development and evaluation strategy than the current more informal methods?

(4) How, if at all, would the character of answerable questions change with alternative multistage selection strategies and randomized trials forming the basis for program development and evaluation?

It is our hope that questions such as these will stimulate further thought on the many subtle aspects of program evaluation where self-selection processes are a central feature.

Acknowledgments. This research was supported by the National Institutes of Health under Grant No. NIH-1-R01-HD16846-01. It is a pleasure to thank Drs. Vincent P. Dole, Alvan Feinstein, and Margaret Marini for stimulating discussions, criticisms, and suggestions on an earlier draft.

Bibliography

Action Committee Against Narcotics. (1981). *Hong Kong Narcotics Report.*

Brook, R.C. and Whitehead, P.C. (1980). *Drug-Free Therapeutic Community.* New York: Human Sciences Press.

Dole, V.P. (1972*a*). "Comments on 'heroin maintenance'." *J. Amer. Med. Assoc.,* 220, 1493.

Dole, V.P. (1972*b*). "Detoxification of sick addicts in prison." *J. Amer. Med. Assoc.,* 220, 366–369.

Dole, V.P. (1980). "Addictive behavior." *Scient. Amer.,* 243, 138–154.

Dole, V.P. and Joseph H. (1979). *Long Term Consequences of Methadone Maintenance Treatment.* New York: Community Treatment Foundation. (Final report under Contract 5 H81 DA 01778-02.)

Dole, V.P. and Nyswander, M.E. (1965). "A medical treatment for diacetylmorphine (heroin) addiction." *J. Amer. Med. Assoc.,* 193, 646–650.

Dole, V.P. and Nyswander, M.E. (1968). "Methadone maintenance and its implications for theories of heroin addiction." In *The Addictive States.* Association for Research in Nervous and Mental Disease, Vol. XLVI, 359–366.

Dole, V.P. and Singer, B. (1979). "On the evaluation of treatments for narcotics addiction." *J. Drug Issues,* 9(2), 205–211

Dole, V.P., Nyswander, M.E., and Kreek, M.J. (1966), "Narcotic blockade." *Arch. Intern. Med.,* 118, 304–309.

Dole, V.P., Nyswander, M.E., DesJarlais, D., and Joseph, H. (1982). "Performance-based ratings of methadone maintenance programs." *New England J. Med.,* 306, 169–172.

DuPont, R.L. (1971). "Profile of a heroin-addiction epidemic." *New England J. Med.,* 285(6), 320–324.

Feinstein, A. (1985). *Clinical Epidemiology.* Philadelphia: W.B. Saunders.

Finney, D.J. (1984). "Improvement by planned multistage selection." *J. Amer. Statist. Assoc.,* 79(387), 501–509.

Gunne, L.-M. (1983). "The case of the Swedish methadone maintenance treatment programme." *Drug and Alcohol Dependence,* 11, 99–103.

Gunne, L.-M. and Gronbladh, L. (1981). "A Swedish methadone maintenance program: A controlled study." *Drug and Alcohol Dependence,* 7, 249–256.

Heckman, J.J. and Robb, R. (1985). "Alternative methods for evaluating the impact of interventions." In J. Heckman and B. Singer (eds.), *Longitudinal Analysis of Labor Market Data.* New York: Cambridge University Press.

Newman, R.G. (1977). *Methadone Treatment in Narcotic Addiction.* New York: Academic Press.

Newman, R.G. (1984). "Testimony before the Senate Subcommittee on Alcoholism and Drug Abuse." 98th Congress, 2nd Session, Committee on Labor and Human Resources, United States Senate, S.HRG. 98-778, 44–60.

Newman, R.G. and Whitehill, W.B. (1979). "Double-blind comparison of methadone and placebo maintenance treatments of narcotics addicts in Hong Kong." *Lancet,* 2, 485–488.

Newman, R.G., Tytum, A., and Bashkow, S. (1976). "Retention of patients in the New York City Methadone Maintenance Treatment Program." *Int. J. Addictions,* 11, 905–931.

Olsson, B., Carlsson, G., Fant, M., Johansson, T., Olsson, O., and Roth, C. (1981). "Heavy drug abuse in Sweden 1979—A national case-finding study in Sweden." *Drug and Alcohol Dependence*, 7, 273–283.

Robins, L.N., Helzer, J.E., and Davis, D.H. (1975). "Narcotic use in southeast Asia and afterward." *Arch. Gen. Psychiatry*, 32, 955–961.

Vaillant, G.E. (1966a). "A 12 year follow-up of New York narcotic addicts: I. The relation of treatment to outcome." *Am. J. Psychiatry*, 122, 727–737.

Vaillant, G.E. (1966b). "A 12 year follow-up of New York narcotic addicts: II. The natural history of a chronic disease." *New England J. Med.*, 275, 1282–1288.

Vaillant, G.E. (1966c). "A 12 year follow-up of New York narcotic addicts: III. Some social and psychiatric characteristics." *Arch. Gen. Psychiatry*, 15, 599–609.

Vaillant, G.E. (1966d). "A 12 year follow-up of New York narcotic addicts: IV. Some determinants and characteristics of abstinence." *Am. J. Psychiatry*, 123, 573–584.

Vaillant, G.E. (1973). "A 20 year follow-up of New York narcotic addicts." *Arch. Gen. Psychiatry*, 29, 237–241.

Discussion 2: Self-Selection and Performance-Based Ratings: A Case Study in Program Evaluation

DISCUSSANT: JOHN HARTIGAN

I'd like to congratulate Burt on the really brilliant display of graphics and data. I'm rather pleased to see none of those fancy Bell Labs type that always make the rest of us feel envious. Moreover, I can't think of a graphics package that could do routinely anything like what Burt has done. Burt has presented an enormous amount of data about a complex problem and really covered all kinds of questions. The unusual combination of text and symbols and figures is especially important. Most graphics packages can draw lines and symbols and things, but they generally fall down on the kind of combination shown here. Yet that's just what you want to see. I do really admire the graphics and display—I think it was excellent.

Now having said all that, I wish I could say something about how you measure the success of drug programs. I guess nearly all of the studies that we saw certainly had tremendous self-selection problems associated with them. The people enter the clinics, they drop out when they please, they come back when they please. Moreover, I'm sure nearly all of those clinics are dependent on showing that they do well in order to continue funding, so I imagine that there's all kinds of statistical cheating going on; people who drop out are converted from one category to another, etc. If I were evaluating the clinics, rather than worry about randomized trials, I'd worry first about how many of these are lying and how can we stop them from lying.

Now is there any way we can think of observational studies that might make for more rational evaluations? It's really so hard to tell. Is this treatment one or treatment two? For example, is a treatment whereby you allow the addicts a rather high level of dosage better than a treatment where you allow no dose at all. Or a treatment in which you allow them a rather high level versus a moderate level. Which one of those do you prefer to use? You might be able to advocate that the clinics would do something like that. After all, it's a matter of disagreement at government levels which is the best thing. Maybe you can't say absolutely "give the addicts everything they want" or "give them nothing at all," but you could get the treatments somewhat closer together in their effect on the addicts. Then, since the treatments would not seem to be too different, randomly assign two groups and follow them for awhile. I wonder if that's really out of the question? I know that the other edge of this is that if you make them that close, then it's going to take a lot of time to really tell the difference.

SINGER: There aren't enough clinics so that you can tell the difference.

HARTIGAN: I suspect that my suggestions may be perfectly futile because I don't really know enough about it. I'm just trying to think, from a statistical point of view, what you could do to collect data that would give some validity to the answers. One other possibility, even in observational studies, would be to compare clinics which for some period of time instituted different policies. You can imagine, as a matter of course, that different clinics will have different policies. Of course, the clinics will have different intake populations too and that's always going to make things difficult, but you could look at two clinics who have different styles of direction (perhaps one has counseling and another doesn't) and do an observational study in which you try to adjust for the different intake populations by regression techniques. That might be effective.

Well, I don't need to keep on going. My feeling is I think Burt has done a masterful job of presenting the problem. I don't feel that I can do an equally masterful job in presenting any solutions. I really feel I can't say much more. John will know. John knows the answers.

DISCUSSANT: JOHN W. TUKEY

The thing we have to adhere to in this group, I think, is that if the information isn't there, we don't try to say it is. It seems to me what Burt told us is that to be sensible, you have to make up your mind what mixture of permanent treatment and short-term treatment you're going to think about and the permanent treatment has to be at least as bad as the diabetic situation. There's some history of just how much trouble you can get into when you're on a diabetic treatment program; where you're running on a more accessible part of a socioeconomic scale.

I don't see how better data extraction can help *very* much. It seems to me the message from your large conglomerate study was that what matters is how long the people stay on the program and that, under the present rules, no one can run a program where success isn't represented by staying on the program for two years.

SINGER: In the U.S. that's true.

TUKEY: Have you not been telling us that the most sensible trial is to try to see how long people stay on the program? If you could reach a couple of years that ought to be taken as a fairly encouraging factor.

SINGER: The Hong Kong trial only ran about a year and a half, but the Rockefeller hospital experience ran roughly 20 years.

TUKEY: What portion of the original group is still alive and on drugs?

SINGER: 75%, and there's a followup on that population going on right now.

TUKEY: So of all the people who have been on long treatment in the world, most of them were in the Rockefeller experiment.

SINGER: Yes. However, just to sustain them, you periodically have to propose that you're going to do a new kind of study, with emphasis on the word "new." Only if you propose that can you get federal approval to do it. A piece of it is to continue the drug administration, but it has to be window dressed with new counseling so that it looks sufficiently different. That's the only way they've been able to sustain their population.

HARTIGAN: I'd like to question whether or not you really do seek to keep the people a long time. Maybe that is correct. Programs might have goals that say "unless you stay off heroin you can't stay in the study." If so, then when you look at people who have been in the study a long time you will find that they're not on heroin. I'm arguing that there's no evidence from what we've seen that being on the program for a long time is the thing that helps you stay off heroin. That's just the way you get into the statistics.

SINGER: Your objection would apply to a very special population. Those that are in the Rockefeller sample were admitted if they had four to five years of daily use when we first started in 1965. Those that are still off it now must attest to the efficacy of the program. You have to agree that's quite a different kettle of fish.

HARTIGAN: Suppose you do a real random experiment in which you keep these same people on for 60 days and others on for 120 days. Then you do some before-and-after addiction rates. I don't see any evidence in the figures so far that the second group would be doing better than the first group. I think the reason that we're seeing the figures as they are is that they are observational studies, and as long as the program administrators have steps available to turn persistent users out of the group, then the guys who've been there a long time are going to show up well in the statistics. So I don't think it's evident.

TUKEY: Well, the fact that, in the Rockefeller experiment, 75% of the group survived over 20 years says there hasn't been much of that going on.

SINGER: That's right. There was temporarily, very early on, users that were going back to heroin. It was only for a maximum of a month or so until they voluntarily came back.

TUKEY: You would have expected, with that kind of follow-up in a nonsensitive area, that you probably would have lost 20% anyway, so that the managers haven't thrown out more than 5%. This is a very special case. It's the only long-term case, and it says for the kind of people they recruited 20 years ago, long-term maintenance seems possible. Now, if you have any kind of a program—I don't care whether it's community therapy or methadone or what have you—where it's demonstrable that the people who stay on have a low percentage of heroin use, then it seems to me what needs most to be demonstrated about that program is that it can be continued. This is saying that I'm buying the insulin analog and not the other.

HARTIGAN: Well, if the Vietnam veteran goes directly there, with no treatment whatsoever, they're fine.

SINGER: That's a different population—one year daily use. Chronic use beyond about 3 years really seems to be a different story.

BRAUN: Have you tried to stratify that population in the different treatment programs by some of those characteristics to see how the percentages change?

SINGER: By years of prior daily use? There's a very sharp distinction between the cutoffs. In fact, that was the basis for the statement that was developed: three years seems to make a difference in terms of whether they could go on their own as opposed to really requiring drug attention.

SWINTON: Is it a physiological possibility that they could be on heroin and on methadone at the same time? That is, do they literally take the methadone and shoot up heroin?

SINGER: They might take the methadone and not necessarily use it, but shoot up heroin. The methadone administration is not meant for them to do away from the clinic. They are given a fixed dose which is not high enough to give them the same kind of kick they get from heroin.

SWINTON: So that being on methadone is not a guarantee that you couldn't have taken heroin.

SINGER: Oh no, but those that are on heroin, while at the clinics, tend to be a very small subset. Additionally, you have to keep up with the counseling service. That's the other thing that's really essential—that seems to be the second biggest discriminator. When you maintain counseling and methadone together you really get stabilized and away from this heroin usage set-up.

BRAUN: One thing that puzzles me is that I don't still have a clear idea what success means. John said that just because you've been in a methadone treatment for a year doesn't mean success.

SINGER: But there's a followup afterwards; with the exception of the Rockefeller hospital population, three years has been about the maximum of any attempt at evaluation and it's considered to be indefinitely. Thus, it's exactly like John's general contention about the cancer patients—five years. You'd like to set up as close to what you would call "natural life span" as possible. According to the cancer example, the followup runs five years now, with success being defined as surviving cancer free for that period.

HARTIGAN: One year would be a fine measure of success. I think what Henry is getting at is he would regard as success someone who goes on the program and stays on it for one year. After all, they're off the streets for one year—that's a kind of success.

BRAUN: I'm saying that's one version of success. Part of the discussion is reflecting that we're not all talking about the same kind of success.

QUESTION FROM AUDIENCE: I don't want to sound cynical, but what is the point of doing a better evaluation? What's going to be the outcome of that?

SINGER: One of the major reasons for pushing for these evaluations is to make a case against regulation of the clinics. The strongest skeptics have said we've never made any scientific evaluation, where the definition of "scientific" (at least within the precincts of the clinical medicine community) means running randomized double blind trials. So lacking any study of that kind in the United States, we have to ask how close can we get before we've got something we can sell? The principal reason for wanting to do this as sharply as possible is to cut back on the regulations a bit.

COMMENT FROM AUDIENCE: It sounds like a political situation—the people who regulate you are the same ones who, in some sense, prevent you from conducting a reasonable evaluation.

SINGER: Yes, it's irrational, there's no question about it.

QUESTION FROM AUDIENCE: Wouldn't you want also to pursue a similar question regarding the efficacy of control substance administration of methadone versus heroin? What would be the objection to a study comparing the two?

SINGER: You can't control the concentration of heroin in a steady range without giving rise to the strong drug-seeking effects which are generally called narcotic effects. There's no range within which you can really stabilize someone with heroin, preventing withdrawal. There's been no record of real success with stabilization.

TUKEY: Didn't you say that the methadone effect has less of a peak and lasts longer? You can do methadone on a longer time interval than you could possibly do heroin.

SINGER: That's right.

QUESTION FROM AUDIENCE: But heroin addicts find heroin sufficiently frequently to maintain themselves in the outside world. What would be wrong with administering it on that same frequency?

TUKEY: The cost for addicts is going to be roughly proportional to how often you have to inject.

COMMENT FROM AUDIENCE: But it's very costly for society to have them administering their own program.

TUKEY: All this is not a case in favor of using heroin instead of methadone. The argument is that methadone is cheaper than heroin, so we can forget the heroin alternative; it's been done.

HARTIGAN: The difference between heroin and methadone is that these guys *want* to use heroin. If you had a heroin clinic you would have no trouble getting customers. It's been tried; in England they do this and it's very successful. You can get as much heroin as you want from the government.

BRAUN: But one of the criteria for success is not only maintenance, but also stable employment. That might be much more difficult with the heroin.

HARTIGAN: My plan is to employ them in the heroin clinics administering heroin. This would take the self-administered operation out of the private sector and into the public sector.

Discussion 3: Alternative Methods for Evaluating the Impact of Intervention

DISCUSSANT: JOHN HARTIGAN

Of course, you'll have to agree that it is a very weird thing you're proposing. You wouldn't want to go on public TV saying this.

I think in principle one has to have doubts about assumptions that you can't check. I'm not quite sure which of these you can check or which you can't. In fact, I often have a great deal of trouble when I see the term "expectation." Exactly what kind of thing is it you're expecting? What worries me is that, normally, when you're dealing with statistical assumptions and you have a relatively simple framework, you can think you can separate many of the problems/assumptions in a frequency framework. Now, we Bayesians don't always want to do that, but I think it helps to be able to say what the population would be over which you take that expectation. I have a feeling that, at least for the cross-sectional data, you're thinking of taking the expectation across the group of individuals who would be considered for training. For understanding the cross-sectional, you should get rid of the t's entirely. You don't really use them. That would simplify things.

HECKMAN: They provide an added degree of generality.

HARTIGAN: That's exactly why I want to take it out—it's an added degree of generality. So why have it in there?

HECKMAN: In some of the discussions, there are repeated cross sections.

HARTIGAN: But for the problems surrounding cross-sectional studies, I don't think you need the added term t. You could check that expectation by averaging across individuals. Now I'm just wondering in this particular case how you would check an assumption by averaging the error across these individuals. Could you check that the error distribution is symmetric?

HECKMAN: Anytime you can check normality, you can also test symmetry.

HARTIGAN: Hang on a second. Let's just suppose that you want to test that it's normal with some estimated mean and variance one. The way you would normally do it is estimate the mean, subtract it out, and then test for symmetry. In this case you can't estimate the mean unless you assume symmetry. Here you can only estimate the mean by cockamamie calculations on polynomials. You can only estimate it when you assume symmetry. So if you go and estimate it, then go and test whether there is symmetry, you are involved in quite a circular enterprise.

HECKMAN: You can't do it without some minimal identifying assumptions —it would not be testable. But if you assume normality, there would be some overidentifying aspects. I don't understand your point about testing these identifying assumptions because I don't see how you can, after you get down to the bare-bones minimum.

HARTIGAN: Shouldn't we all identify which assumptions aren't testable? I would like to complete my remarks with a rather unpointed comment—that is, someone told me very recently about an architect, a surgeon, and economist. The surgeon said, "Look, we're the most important. God's a surgeon because the very first thing that God did was to extract Eve from Adam's rib." The architect said, "No, wait a minute, God is an architect. God made the world in seven days out of chaos." The economist smiled, "And who made the chaos?"

DISCUSSANT: JOHN W. TUKEY

Well, I think I have to begin with a remark that, as a data analyst (which I am most of the time), this is helping to convince me that economists are even more theoretical than statisticians. I got to feeling very unhappy when the idea was "well, of course, we can assume that things are polynomials of degree $n - 2$." I'm not sure whether I believe in the real existence of polynomials of larger than the second degree. Did you ever see the paper by Norbert Wiener which includes the definition "a continuous polynomial chaos" is a function of n variables such that da de da de da? I think it's always dangerous to think about polynomials of more than a minimum degree. I'm not trying to say the world is linear, but I'm trying to say that the idea that we know what it's like when it isn't is probably wrong.

I'm clearly speaking in broad generalities, the way John Hartigan did. I believe for the same reasons. In my case it might be more honest to say because there have been enough equations to make my eyes bug out. But I think an important point that we have to come back to at intervals is that knowledge always comes from a combination of data and assumptions. If the assumptions are too important, many of us get unhappy. I think one thing we were told in this last discussion was that all the formal ways that have been found for attacking this problem ended up being very dependent upon these assumptions. Therefore, people like me have to be very uncomfortable about the results. There's some sort of question about the continuity of knowledge—continuity in the assumptions. If it were really true that Student's t only worked when the world followed the Gaussian distribution, then Student would have never earned any reputation and nobody would use Student's t.

Over a range of things, quite a distance from the Gaussian actually, Student's t does work pretty well. It may not be efficient, but from the point of view of what you were talking about here, it is conservative—the things you think of as positive assertions you can usually believe in—unless you have a relatively short tail. And while nobody that I know of can prove that anything is exactly Gaussian, in the simplest problems you can have some idea of the distribution and often you can be sure it isn't short tailed.

We seem to be getting a message here that things depend upon the assumption being sharply correct. It matters whether something is *really* an instrument, it matters whether or not the third and fifth moments vanish exactly, etc. It seems to me that such reliance on *precise* assumptions is dangerous.

Let me come back to a related point: I'm not clear enough about this sort of model to know to what extent non-financial motivations have serious impact on what's going to happen if you try to use them. Now it seems to me that anticipated social status is a major motivation for a substantial segment of the population, for why people are training. People go to be doctors because their parents think doctors are in the upper crust and they'd like to see their children rise. Whether or not they make more money (in this particular case) I doubt makes much difference because they're going to make more money anyway. Is this the sort of thing that you would cover with the unobservables? You hope it behaves all right. To the extent that ethnic groups are systematically different in this regard, you suggest that maybe some ethnic-group stratifications might offer some insight.

I don't think you've done your duty by saying what is consistent and what is not. I don't want to push you into detailed revisions, but I think it might be fair to try to think about prototype problems in asking, "What power of ten do you need in data in order for this assertion to give a certain general sort of precision?" The argument was "the efficiencies are higher for the longitudinal; they may be better, but the data cost a lot more." Qualitatively, I think that's a good argument. Quantitatively, I'd like to know whether I need, say, a hundred, ten thousand, or a million times as much data to balance out. That's in factors of a hundred; I'd like to come down to factors of ten. I don't think I need to ask for factors of two. My guess is that the fifth moment calculation requires a factor of a 100 times as much data as to run only the third one and live with the three roots. If that's about right, it helps us a lot in thinking about the problem. So I would encourage you to do some more on the harder questions and get even rough ideas of what consistency means in terms of an estimate that maybe you wouldn't want to put on public television, but you might be willing to put on the bulletin board in the economics department.

I think this business of checking up needs to be taken a lot more seriously. Let me illustrate an instance. If you took a particular set of data where you never ground the numbers through anything and you had even a general idea of the distribution of things, I would not be surprised if there were 8 to 10 questions for which there were 2 reasonable answers to how you're going to analyze them. Is this thing Gaussian or is its logarithm

Gaussian? Or is its square root Gaussian? Is this a good instrument? Is that a good instrument/assumption? I would like to see the 2^8 to 2^{10} (256 to 1024) alternative calculations made and get some idea of what is the distribution of the answers. I think at that point you'd find yourself inevitably focusing on what are the crucial questions that that procedure revealed. Until people start doing that, rather than doing only one or admitting to doing only one, I think large opportunities are being missed.

There is one real difficulty with the models in general which I don't quite see how you attack. If because there was a large United Nations grant available to provide food and shelter so that everybody in the country took off from their regular jobs for a year and took a particular sort of training, would this raise any of their incomes in the future? I think it dubious. I think that the relationship of the financial impact of training to the percentage of the population trained has eventually got to come in. It's very difficult to see how—I'm not trying to say you're foolish if you haven't done this. I'm trying to say that in extreme cases you can get in trouble. Maybe it's time to start thinking about it. Finally, I want to say that the last set of words the last speaker said before he sat down were, on the whole, quite wise.

HECKMAN: There were a number of points and I enjoyed them all. On the question of the financial motivation—we didn't discuss the enrollment rules, but there are a variety of different motivations (financial or nonfinancial) that may give rise to the selection process. We offered one example in the handout although we didn't discuss it. But certainly we're not tied to any type of specific model of the choice process for some of the estimators. That's a crucial thing. Social scientists give the greatest heat exactly about how precisely you are specifying enrollment. What are the determinants of those rules? One should be quite loose about specifying those considerations.

On the question about the sharpness, it may be a limitation imposed by the kind of objectives we set for ourselves. Identification is a sharp thing, and I'm fully sympathetic with the idea that one wants to be more broad.

TUKEY: The idea of identification is sort of an ideally sharp thing and somehow, in the real world, hard to deal with.

HECKMAN: I grant that point. In some sense, by focusing as narrowly as we have, we appear to be making some very sharp conclusions. In practice, however, (although I know nothing at this point since some of these estimators haven't been tried out on a data set) I would imagine that one can probably live with some slack—some departure from some of these assumptions—but I simply don't know. It's a real defect in the paper as we've written it. Although I think it may also be an asset, in the sense that we really do have sharpness as an objective. I can't believe the world is going to deteriorate completely if the third moment is 10^{-5} instead of zero, but I frankly don't know. That's a good question. The same questions about the various other aspects of the assumptions are still very much open for investigation. Some of these estimators are quite new; the efficiency calculations simply haven't been done yet. That's something that will be done.

TUKEY: I thought you made a good argument why it can't be done.

HECKMAN: It can within specific limited contexts. I agree that for our purpose it can't be done because we really have different dimensions, different data sets, different models that aren't comparable. I think that the question you're raising about the number of observations needed, depending on the fifth moment vis-a-vis the third moment is valid. That is again something that we simply don't know.

HARTIGAN: John, are you trying to encourage them to promulgate that method? Is that what you're hinting at here?

TUKEY: If they were able to conclude, for example, that to make the method go, you'd usually need about 10^{11} observations, I would think that was getting a useful piece of knowledge.

HARTIGAN: The face validity of that method is really very slight. It's unbelievable that it might work.

TUKEY: John, you and I have some feeling, which we would find hard to defend in a room full of economists, as to what sort of sample sizes would be needed to make something of that sort work, even if the assumptions were right. But I don't think we ought to ask them to have that feeling until they look at the problem.

HECKMAN: Would you feel more comfortable if we made a normality assumption?

HARTIGAN: I probably would because I think that you're getting experience in dealing in generality by assuming that higher moments are zero. I would ask you another question: I would say, how would you check the assumptions? I'm frightened that you are going to go away and do a study where you need 10 observations to use the fifth moment. Well, ok, how is it going to work? What do you mean it's going to work? You don't know that the fifth moment is zero. You have no idea. If it's not zero what happens?

HECKMAN: We aren't tying ourselves necessarily to setting the fifth moment to zero. The notion of where you come from is the key to your own excesses. If you come from groups where normality is routinely invoked, you could take that path. It seemed to me that was unnecessary. Our limited objective is asking, what principle do you need? We are truly not advocating its third and fifth moment. I think that would be very hard to defend. Some people might believe in the symmetries of the validity theory, fantasy exercises of the sort that social science people mysticize about. There might be some subset of the community that could actually buy that. Some might be happy with tests; we certainly are not. It goes back to the point raised earlier about sharpness. Sharpness of these assumptions is really a consequence of the nature of the way the paper was written, not the nature of the problem. This obviously requires faith in the nature of continuity and a little loose hoping.

Let me come back to this question that Professor Tukey raised. It is an extremely interesting problem going well outside of here. That is the question about the consequences of these programs when there's some sort of large-scale adjustment. For example, what happens in the evaluations of the negative income tax program and the like? When you come up with microeconomic studies you inevitably ask yourself, what would the consequences of these things be if, in fact, it had some larger scale adjustment? Large-scale participation of a lot of poor people could actually be changing the labor market for the poor people. If everyone participated in training, the information taken from the training program might be much different than if nobody did. There is some research in economics on these questions, but again, I'm afraid that the assumptions required to address these adjustments are brutal. You're really asking how the economy behaves in situations well outside the range of any data, and people are properly agnostic about those assumptions. I think it's a very valid point.

It's also the case in unionism studies. You ask what happens if you go from a labor force that is 1% unionized to one that is 30% unionized? You rapidly change the whole idea of who unionization is likely to attract and even what would be the comparison group earnings. There's an assumption the program is operating in microeconomic isolation.

TUKEY: Let me address these comments to John Hartigan and let you off the hook for the moment. You and I, I think, would feel that a normality assumption used to support Student's t is not too bad. The normality assumption when used to support the idea that s^2/σ^2 is like χ^2/f (leading to an interval for σ^2) is something else. I know what I would say about this, and I'm pretty sure I know what you would say. It's a question of differential sensitivity. I suggest that all of us have a feeling that what people would use normality for in this sort of business has even worse sensitivity than the things we're already throwing in the ashes. So I don't think, when we get down to it, that we can go with your idea, that we buy the normality assumption.

HARTIGAN: I think it's true that if normality is used in a serious way, it can have serious effects on calculations. That is correct. I'm just saying that I suspect that an assumption like "third and fifth moments are zero" is pretty close in its effect to the normality assumption. So that it might be an illusion of progress to retreat from it in this way. I just know in my bones that no one (I hope no economist) is ever going to solve that fifth moment, find the distribution, and say "Aha, here is my estimate of α." If he does, I hope he doesn't tell anyone else about it nor how he did it. Because it couldn't possibly work.

HECKMAN: You're whetting my appetite.

TUKEY: I think we have to admit this is a matter of sample size. If you go up to statistical mechanics where the 10^{21} is a small sample size, it might work.

HARTIGAN: I would agree that if you got 10^{21} you work on it to figure out a few more things about whether or not its third and fifth moment are exactly zero before you can do some things. With 10^{21} observations, you probably know a bit more about the distribution.

TUKEY: It does help.

Alternative Methods for Solving the Problem of Selection Bias in Evaluating the Impact of Treatments on Outcomes

JAMES J. HECKMAN AND RICHARD ROBB

I. Introduction

Social scientists *never* have access to true experimental data of the type sometimes available to laboratory scientists.[1] Our inability to use laboratory methods to independently vary treatments to eliminate or isolate spurious channels of causation places a fundamental limitation on the possibility of objective knowledge in the social sciences. In place of laboratory experimental variation, social scientists use subjective thought experiments. Assumptions replace data. In the jargon of modern econometrics, minimal identifying assumptions are invoked.

Because minimal identifying assumptions cannot be tested with data (all possible minimal assumptions for a model explain the observed data equally well, at least in large samples) and because empirical estimates of causal relationships are sensitive to these assumptions, inevitably there is scope for disagreement in the causal interpretation of social science data. Context, beliefs, and *a priori* theory resolve differences in causal interpretations (see Simon, 1957, for an early statement of this view). By definition, the available data cannot do so, although in principle, experiments can.[2] The solution to the problem of causal inference lies outside of mathematical statistics and depends on contexts which are not universal.

The problem of selection bias in the analysis of social science data is a special case of the general problem of causal inference from social science

---

[1] That the recently conducted so called social experiments are not laboratory experiments is abundantly clear from the literature on the topic. See, e.g., Fienberg et al. (1985) and the references cited therein.

[2] The second remark in this sentence abstracts from the very real problems of designing or conducting true social experiments. Self selection by agents (including attrition) and the vast multiplicity of possible channels of causal influence make experimentation problematic if not infeasible. Alleged solutions to the problems of self selection and attrition based on arbitrary normality assumptions *inject* into the analysis of experimental data subjective features which the experiments were proposed to avoid.

data. This paper considers alternative assumptions that have been or might
be invoked to solve the problem of causal inference created by selection
bias. In this paper we consider the following topics.

First, we define selection bias and the "structural" or causal parameters
of interest for the following prototypical model. Persons are given (or else
select) "treatments," but the assignment of persons to treatments is nonrandom. Differences in measured outcomes among persons are due to the
treatment and to factors that would make people different on outcome
measures even if there were no causal effect of the treatment. "Treatment,"
as we use the term, may be a drug trial, a training program, attending
school, joining a union, or migrating to a region. For specificity, in this
paper we consider a training program but only because it provides a
convenient prototypical context against which it is possible to gauge the
plausibility of certain identifying assumptions. Except for this contextual
content, our analysis is applicable to all of the other treatments mentioned
above. We assume that it is not possible to simultaneously observe the same
person in the treated and untreated states. If it is possible to observe the
same person in both states, the problem of selection bias disappears.[3] By
observing the same person in the treated and untreated states, it is possible
to isolate the treatment in question without having to invoke any further
assumptions.

A careful definition of the causal or structural parameter of interest is an
essential aspect of this paper. The literature in social science is unclear on
this issue. Conventional "average treatment" definitions often used in the
statistics literature (see, e.g., Rosenbaum and Rubin, 1983) often do not
define the parameter of interest to behavioral social scientists.

A second topic considered in this paper is the specification of minimal
identifying assumptions required to isolate the parameters of interest. We
consider the plausibility of these assumptions in the context of well-for-
mulated models of the impact of training on earnings.

We present assumptions required to use three types of widely available
data to solve the problem of estimating the impact of training on earnings
free of selection bias: (1) a single cross section of post-training earnings, (2)
a temporal sequence of cross sections of unrelated people (repeated cross-
section data), and (3) longitudinal data in which the same individuals are
followed over time. These three types of data are listed in order of their
availability and in inverse order of their cost of acquisition. If we assume
that random sampling techniques are applied to collect all three types of
data, then the three sources form a hierarchy: longitudinal data can be used
to generate a single cross section or a set of repeated cross sections in which
the identities of individuals are ignored, and repeated cross sections can be
used as single cross sections.

---

[3] The Glynn et al. paper (this volume) essentially makes this assumption and thus assumes
away selection bias in the mixture modeling section.

Our conclusions are rather startling. Although longitudinal data are widely regarded in the social science and statistical communities as a panacea for selection and simultaneity problems, there is no need to use longitudinal data to identify the impact of training on earnings if conventional specifications of earnings functions are adopted.[4] Estimators based on repeated cross-section data for unrelated persons identify the same parameter. This is true for virtually all longitudinal estimators.

However, in this paper we question the plausibility of conventional specifications. They are not often motivated by any behavioral theory, and when examined in the light of a plausible theory, conventional specifications seem poorly motivated. We propose richer longitudinal specifications of the earnings process and enrollment decision derived from behavioral theory. In addition, we propose a variety of new estimators. A few of these estimators require longitudinal data, but for most, such data are not required. A major conclusion of our paper is that the relative benefits of longitudinal data have been overstated because the potential benefits of cross-section and repeated cross-section data have been understated.

When minimal identifying assumptions are explored for models fit on the three types of data, we find that *different* and not necessarily more plausible assumptions can be invoked in longitudinal analyses than in cross-section and repeated cross-section analyses. The fact that more types of minimal identifying assumptions can be invoked with longitudinal data (since the longitudinal data can be used as a cross section or a repeated cross section) does not make more plausible those assumptions that uniquely exploit longitudinal data.

In analyzing the assumptions required to use various data sources to consistently estimate the impact of training on earnings free of selection bias, we discuss the following topics:

(1) How much prior information about the earnings function must be assumed?
(2) How much prior information about the decision rule governing participation must be assumed?
(3) How robust are the proposed methods to the following commonly encountered features of data on training?

    (a) nonrandomness of available samples and especially oversampling of trainees (the choice-based sample problem);
    (b) time inhomogeneity in the environment ("nonstationarity"); and
    (c) the absence of a control group of nontrainees or the contamination of the control group so that the training status of individuals is not known for the control sample.

---

[4] Conventional specifications include "fixed effect" or "autoregressive" assumptions for the error terms of earnings equations. These terms are defined below.

We also question recent claims of the sort made in the paper by Glynn et al. (this volume) which state that cross-section approaches to solving the problem of selection bias are strongly dependent on arbitrary assumptions about distributions of unobservables and on certain arbitrary exclusion restrictions (see also Little, 1985, where such claims are also made). While some widely used cross-section estimators suffer from this defect, such commonly invoked assumptions are not an essential feature of the cross-section approach, at least for the type of selection problem considered in this paper. However, we demonstrate that unless explicit distributional assumptions are invoked, all cross-section estimators require the presence of at least one regressor variable in the decision rule determining training. This requirement may seem innocuous, but it rules out a completely nonparametric cross-section approach. Without prior information, it is not possible to cross-classify observations on the basis of values assumed by explanatory variables in the earnings function and do "regressor-free" estimation of the impact of training on earnings that is free of selection bias. A regressor is required in the equation determining enrollment. Without a regressor it is necessary to invoke distributional assumptions. Longitudinal and repeated cross-section estimators do not require a regressor.

A third topic considered in this paper is an assessment of both the "mixture modeling" approach to the selection bias problem advocated by Glynn et al. (this volume) and the propensity score methodology of Rosenbaum and Rubin (1983, 1985) that has been advocated as an alternative to selection bias procedures by Coleman (1985) and Scheuren (1985). We make two points. First, under the Glynn et al. assumptions about the data-generating mechanism, there is no real problem of selection bias. Those authors assume access to data on participants and nonparticipants which when appropriately weighted can produce unbiased estimates of treatment impact. Such data are typically not available. Second, propensity score methods solve the selection bias problem only in special cases that often turn out to be behaviorally uninteresting. The propensity score is not a panacea or genuine alternative methodology for general selection bias problems.

The focus of this paper is on model identification and not on estimation or on the efficiency of alternative estimators. As noted by Tukey in his discussion of this paper, identification is a rather sharp concept that may not be all that helpful a guide to what will "work" in practice. Different estimators may perform quite differently in practice depending on the degree of overidentification or on the nature of the identifying restriction. However, if a parameter is not identified, an estimator of that parameter cannot have any desirable statistical properties. Securing identification is a necessary first step toward construction of a desirable estimator, but certainly is not the last step. This paper concentrates on the necessary first step.

Our focus on identification and on the tradeoffs in assumptions that secure identification should make clear that we are not offering a nostrum for selection bias that "works" in all cases. In our view, the recent literature on this subject has been marred by analysts who claim to offer context-free universal cures for the selection problem. There are almost as many cures as there are contexts, and for that reason no one cure can be said to "work" for all problems.[5]

We focus on identification because the current literature in social science and statistics is unclear on this topic. A major goal of this paper is to demonstrate that previous work on selection bias has often imposed unnecessarily strong assumptions (e.g., normality). Part of the great variability in estimates obtained in some analyses using selection bias procedures may be due to the imposition of different types of extra conditions not required to identify the parameters of interest. Separating out essential from inessential assumptions is a main goal of this paper.

The way we have written this paper may cause some confusion. We establish identifiability by establishing the existence of consistent estimators. Thus, we combine two topics that might fruitfully be decoupled. By establishing the consistency of a variety of estimators, we present a large sample guide to estimation under a variety of assumptions. However, the price of this approach to model identification is that we invoke assumptions not strictly required for identification alone (see Barros, 1986, where this type of separation of assumptions is done). Fewer assumptions are required for identification than are required for consistent estimation. As noted by Tukey in his written comments on this paper, clarity would be served if the reader mentally substituted "c-identified" (for consistency identified) for "identified" everywhere the subject of identification is discussed in this paper.

We have already noted that we use large sample theory in our analysis. Given the size of many social science data sets with hundreds and thousands of independent observations and given the available Monte Carlo evidence, large sample methods are not unreliable. For these reasons, we view our large sample analysis as the natural point of departure for research on selection models.

We do not discuss efficiency or variance questions in this paper. A discussion of efficiency makes sense only within the context of a fully specified model. The focus in this paper is on the tradeoffs in assumptions that must be imposed to estimate a single coefficient when the analyst has access to different types of data. Since different assumptions about the underlying model are invoked to justify the validity of alternative estimators, an efficiency or sampling variance comparison is often meaningless. Under the assumptions about an underlying model that justify one estima-

---

[5]Except, of course, the cure of genuine experimental data.

tor, properties of another estimator may not be defined. Only by postulating a common assumption set that is unnecessarily large for any single estimator is it possible to make efficiency comparisons. For the topic of this paper—model identification—the efficiency issue is a red herring.

Even if a common set of assumptions about the underlying model is invoked to justify efficiency comparisons for a class of estimators, conventional efficiency comparisons are often meaningless for two reasons. First, the frequently stated claim that longitudinal estimators are more efficient than cross-section estimators is superficial. It ignores the relative sizes of the available cross-section and longitudinal samples. Because of the substantially greater cost of collecting longitudinal data free of attrition bias, the number of persons followed in longitudinal studies rarely exceeds 500 in most social science analyses. In contrast, the available cross-section and repeated cross-section samples have thousands of observations. Given the relative sizes of the available cross-section and longitudinal samples, "inefficient" cross-section and repeated cross-section estimators might have much smaller sampling variances than "efficient" longitudinal estimators that are fit on much smaller samples. In this sense, our proposed cross-section and repeated cross-section estimators might be feasibly efficient given the relative sizes of the samples for the two types of data sources. However, we do not analyze this topic further in our paper.

Second, many of the cross-section and repeated cross-section estimators proposed in this paper require only sample means of variables. They are thus very simple to compute and are also robust to mean zero measurement error in all of the variables. Some more sophisticated longitudinal and cross-section estimators are computationally complex and in practice are often implemented on only a fraction of the available data to save computing cost. Simple methods based on means use all of the data and thus, in practice, might be more efficient.

Barros (1986) presents a very thorough discussion of the efficiency issue for alternative selection estimators for cases where the concept is well defined.

This paper draws heavily on our previous work (Heckman and Robb, 1985). To avoid repetition and to focus on essential points, we refer the reader to our longer companion paper for technical details of certain arguments. However, we use this paper to correct some minor typographical and conceptual errors that appeared in our previous work.

The organization of this paper is as follows. Section II describes the notation and a behavioral model of the enrollment of persons into training. Section III discusses the definition of the appropriate causal or structural parameter of interest. Sections IV–IX present a discussion of alternative estimation methods for different types of data. Section X discusses "mixture modeling" and "propensity score" methods as solutions to the selection bias problems considered in this paper and relates the propensity score method to techniques developed in the econometrics literature. Propensity score methods are demonstrated to solve only a special and not very interesting case of the general selection bias problem.

II. Notation and a Model of Program Participation

A. Earnings Functions

To focus on essential aspects of the problem, we assume that individuals experience only one opportunity to participate in training. This opportunity occurs in period k. Training takes a single period for participants to complete. During training, participants earn no labor income.

Denote the latent earnings of individual i in period t by Y_{it}^*. These are the earnings of an individual in the absence of the existence of any training programs. Latent earnings depend on a vector of observed characteristics X_{it}. Let U_{it} represent the error term in the latent earnings equation and assume that

$$E(U_{it}|X_{it}) = 0.$$

Adopting a linear specification, we write latent earnings as

$$Y_{it}^* = X_{it}\beta + U_{it},$$

where β is a vector of parameters. Linearity is adopted only as a convenient starting point and is not an essential aspect of any of the methods presented in this paper. Throughout this paper we assume that the mean of U_{it} given X_{it} is the same for all X_{it}. Sometimes we will require independence between X_{it} and current, future, and lagged values of U_{it}. When X_{it} contains lagged values of Y_{it}^*, we assume that the equation for Y_{it}^* can be solved for a reduced form expression involving only exogenous regressor variables. Under standard conditions, it is possible to estimate the structure from the reduced form so defined.

Under these assumptions, β is the coefficient of X in the conditional expectation of Y^* given X. Observed earnings Y_{it} are related to latent earnings Y_{it}^* in the following way:

$$Y_{it} = Y_{it}^* + d_i\alpha \qquad t > k$$
$$Y_{it} = Y_{it}^* \qquad\qquad t \leq k,$$

where $d_i = 1$ if the person takes training and $d_i = 0$ otherwise and where α is one definition of the causal or structural effect of training on earnings. Observed earnings are the sum of latent earnings and the structural shift term $d_i\alpha$ that is a consequence of training. Y_{it} is thus the sum of two random variables when $t > k$.

The problem of selection bias arises because d_i may be correlated with U_{it}. This is a consequence of selection decisions by agents. Thus, selection bias is present if

$$E(U_{it}d_i) \neq 0.$$

Observed earnings may be written as

$$Y_{it} = X_{it}\beta + d_i\alpha + U_{it} \qquad t > k$$
$$Y_{it} = X_{it}\beta + U_{it} \qquad\qquad t \le k,$$

(1)

where β and α are parameters. Because of the covariance between d_i and U_{it},

$$E(Y_{it}|X_{it}, d_i) \ne X_{it}\beta + d_i\alpha.$$

Equation (1) assumes that training has the same effect on everyone. In the next section we consider issues that arise when α varies among individuals, as is assumed in many analyses of experimental and nonexperimental data (see Fisher, 1953; Rosenbaum and Rubin, 1983). Throughout most of this paper we ignore effects of training which grow or decay over time (see our companion paper for a discussion of this topic).

We now develop the stochastic relationship between d_i and U_{it} in equation (1). For this purpose, we present a more detailed notation which describes the enrollment rules that select individuals into training.

B. Enrollment Rules

The decision to participate in training may be determined by a prospective trainee, by a program administrator, or both. Whatever the specific content of the rule, it can be described in terms of an index function framework. Let IN_i be an index of net benefits to the appropriate decision makers from taking training. It includes the loss of income in period k if training is taken. It is a function of observed (Z_i) and unobserved (V_i) variables. Thus,

$$IN_i = Z_i\gamma + V_i.$$

(2)

In terms of this function,

$$d_i = 1 \qquad \text{iff} \quad IN_i > 0$$

$$d_i = 0 \qquad \text{otherwise.}$$

The distribution function of V_i is denoted as $F(v_i) = \Pr(V_i < v_i)$. V_i is assumed to be independently and identically distributed across persons. Let $p = E(d_i) = \Pr(d_i = 1)$ and assume $1 > p > 0$. Assuming that V_i is distributed independently of Z_i (a requirement not needed for most of the estimators considered in this paper), we may write $\Pr(d_i = 1|Z_i) = F(-Z_i\gamma)$, which is sometimes called the "propensity score" in statistics (see, e.g., Rosenbaum and Rubin, 1983). In Section X we demonstrate that a special subclass of econometric selection–correction estimators can be expressed as functions of the propensity score.

The condition for the existence of selection bias

$$E(U_{it}d_i) \neq 0$$

may occur because of stochastic dependence between U_{it} and the unobservable V_i in equation (2) (selection on the unobservables) or because of stochastic dependence between U_{it} and Z_i in equation (2) (selection on the observables).

To interpret various specifications of equation (2), we need a behavioral model. A natural starting point is a model of trainee self-selection based on a comparison of the expected value of earnings with and without training. For simplicity, we assume that training programs accept all applicants.[6]

All prospective trainees are assumed to discount earnings streams by a common discount factor of $1/(1 + r)$. Training raises trainee earnings by α per period. While in training, individual i receives a subsidy S_i, which may be negative (so there may be direct costs of program participation). Trainees forego income in training period k. To simplify the expressions, we assume that people live forever.

As of period k, the present value of earnings for a person who does not receive training is

$$PV_i(0) = E_{k-1}\left[\sum_{j=0}^{\infty} \left(\frac{1}{1+r} \right)^j Y^*_{i,k+j} \right].$$

E_{k-1} means that the mathematical expectation is taken with respect to information available to the prospective trainee in period $k - 1$. The expected present value of earnings for a trainee is

$$PV_i(1) = E_{k-1}\left[\sum_{j=1}^{\infty} \left(\frac{1}{1+r} \right)^j Y^*_{i,k+j} + \sum_{j=1}^{\infty} \frac{\alpha}{(1+r)^j} \right].$$

The risk neutral wealth-maximizing decision rule is to enroll in the program if $PV_i(1) > PV_i(0)$ or, letting IN_i denote the index function in the decision rule of equation (2),

$$\text{IN}_i = PV_i(1) - PV_i(0) = E_{k-1}(S_i - Y_{ik} + \alpha/r), \tag{3}$$

so the decision to train is characterized by the rule

$$\begin{aligned} d_i &= 1 \quad \text{iff} \quad E_{k-1}(S_i - Y_{ik} + \alpha/r) > 0 \\ d_i &= 0 \quad \text{otherwise.} \end{aligned} \tag{4}$$

Let W_i be the part of the subsidy which the analyst observes (with associated coefficient ϕ) and let τ_i be the part which he or she does not observe:

$$S_i = W_i\phi + \tau_i.$$

---

[6] Our previous paper considers more general models.

A special case of this model arises when agents possess perfect foresight so that $E_{k-1}(S_i) = S_i$, $E_{k-1}(Y_{ik}) = Y_{ik}$, and $E_{k-1}(\alpha/r) = \alpha/r$. Collecting terms,

$$d_i = 1 \quad \text{iff} \quad S_i - Y_{ik} + \alpha/r = W_i\phi + \alpha/r - X_{ik}\beta + \tau_i - U_{ik} > 0$$
$$d_i = 0 \quad \text{otherwise.} \tag{5}$$

Then $\tau_i - U_{ik} = V_i$ in equation (2) and (W_i, X_{ik}) corresponds to Z_i in equation (2). If we assume that (W_i, X_{ik}) is distributed independently of V_i, then inequalities (5) define a standard discrete choice model. This assumption is only required for some of the estimators discussed in this paper.

Suppose decision rule (5) determines enrollment. If the costs of program participation are independent of U_{it} for all t (so both W_i and τ_i are independent of U_{it}), then $E(U_{it}d_i) = 0$ only if the mean of the unobservables in period t does not depend on the unobservables in period k, or

$$E(U_{it}|U_{ik}) = 0 \quad t > k.$$

Whether or not U_{it} and d_i are uncorrelated hinges on the serial dependence properties of U_{it}. If U_{it} is a moving average of order of m so that

$$U_{it} = \sum_{j=1}^{m} a_j\epsilon_{i,t-j},$$

where $\epsilon_{i,t-j}$ are iid, then for $t - k > m$, $E(U_{it}d_i) = 0$. However, if U_{it} follows a first-order autoregressive scheme, then $E(U_{it}|U_{ik}) \neq 0$ for all t and k.

The enrollment decision rules derived in this subsection give context to the selection bias problem. The estimators discussed in this paper differ greatly in their dependence on particular features of these rules. Some estimators do not require that these decision rules be specified at all, while other estimators require a great deal of *a priori* specification of these rules. Given the inevitable controversy that surrounds specification of enrollment rules, there is always likely to be a preference by analysts for estimators that require little prior knowledge about the decision rule.

III. Random Coefficients and the Structural Parameter of Interest

We identify two different definitions associated with the notion of a selection bias-free estimate of the impact of training on earnings. The first notion defines the structural parameter of interest as the impact of training on earnings if people are randomly assigned to training programs. The second notion defines the structural parameter of interest in terms of the difference between the postprogram earnings of the trained and what the earnings in postprogram years for these same individuals would have been in the absence of training. The two notions come to the same thing only when training has an equal impact on everyone or else assignment to training is random with respect to earnings and attention centers on estimating the mean response to training. The second notion is the most useful one for forecasting future program impacts when the same enrollment rules that have been used in available samples characterize future enrollment.

In seeking to determine the impact of training on earnings in the presence of nonrandom assignment of persons to training, it is useful to distinguish two questions that are frequently confused in the literature.

Question 1: *"What would be the mean impact of training on earnings if people were randomly assigned to training?"*

Question 2: *"How do the postprogram mean earnings of the trained compare to what they would have been in the absence of training?"*

The second question makes a hypothetical contrast between the postprogram earnings of the trained in the presence and in the absence of training programs. This hypothetical contrast eliminates factors that would make the earnings of trainees different from those of nontrainees even in the absence of any training program. The two questions have the same answer if equation (1) generates earnings so that training has the same impact on everyone. The two questions also have the same answer if there is random assignment to training and if attention centers on estimating the *population* mean response to training.

In the presence of nonrandom assignment and variation in the impact of training among persons, the two questions have different answers. Question two is the appropriate one to ask if interest centers on forecasting the change in the mean of the post-training earnings of trainees compared to what *they* would have earned in the absence of training when the same selection rule pertains to past and future trainees. It is important to note that the answer to this question is all that is required to estimate the future program impact if future selection criteria are like past criteria and all that is required is to evaluate the gross return from training (the return exclusive of leisure and direct costs).[7]

To clarify these issues, we consider a random coefficient version of equation (1) in which α varies in the population. In this model, the impact

---

[7]There is a third question that might be asked: "What would be the effect of training on the earnings of the trained if the future selection rule for trainees differs from the past selection rule?" This question is more ambitious than the two stated in the text and requires that more assumptions be made. Given the general interest in questions one and two, we feel that a discussion of the answers to these two questions should precede a discussion of the answer to question three.

of training may differ across persons and may even be negative for some people. We write in place of equation (1)

$$Y_{it} = X_{it}\beta + d_i\alpha_i + U_{it} \qquad t > k.$$

Define $E(\alpha_i) = \bar{\alpha}$ and $\epsilon_i = \alpha_i - \bar{\alpha}$ so $E(\epsilon_i) = 0$. With this notation, we can rewrite the equation above as

$$Y_{it} = X_{it}\beta + d_i\bar{\alpha} + (U_{it} + d_i\epsilon_i). \tag{6}$$

Note that the expected value of the term in parentheses is nonzero. X_{it} is assumed to be independent of (U_{it}, ϵ_i). An alternative way to derive this equation is to express it as a two-sector switching model following Roy (1951), Goldfeld and Quandt (1976), Heckman and Neumann (1977), and Lee (1978). Let

$$Y_{1it} = X_{it}\beta_1 + U_{1it}$$

be the wage of individual i in sector 1 in period t. Let

$$Y_{0it} = X_{it}\beta_0 + U_{0it}$$

be the wage of individual i in sector 0. X_{it} is independent of (U_{1it}, U_{0it}). Let $d_i = 1$ if a person is in sector 1 and let $d_i = 0$ otherwise. We may write the observed wage as

$$
\begin{aligned}
Y_{it} &= d_i Y_{1it} + (1 - d_i) Y_{0it} \\
&= X_{it}\beta_0 + E(X_{it}|d_i = 1)(\beta_1 - \beta_0)d_i \\
&\quad + \{[X_{it} - E(X_{it}|d_i = 1)](\beta_1 - \beta_0) + U_{1it} - U_{0it}\}d_i + U_{0it}.
\end{aligned}
$$

Letting $\bar{\alpha} = E(X_{it}|d_i = 1)(\beta_1 - \beta_0)$, $\epsilon_i = [X_{it} - E(X_{it}|d_i = 1)](\beta_1 - \beta_0) + U_{1it} - U_{0it}$, $\beta_0 = \beta$, and $U_{0it} = U_{it}$, produces equation (6).

In this model there is a fundamental nonidentification result when no regressors appear in the decision rule of equation (2). Without a regressor in equation (2) and in the absence of any further distributional (or moment) assumptions, it is not possible to identify $\bar{\alpha}$ unless $E(\epsilon_i|d_i = 1, Z_i) = 0$ or some other known constant.

To see this, note that

$$E(Y_{it}|d_i = 1, Z_i, X_{it}) = X_{it}\beta + \bar{\alpha} + E(\epsilon_i|d_i = 1, Z_i) + E(U_{it}|d_i = 1, Z_i)$$

$$E(Y_{it}|d_i = 0, Z_i, X_{it}) = X_{it}\beta + E(U_{it}|d_i = 0, Z_i).$$

Unless $E(\epsilon_i|d_i = 1, Z_i)$ is known, without invoking distributional assumptions, it is impossible to decompose $\bar{\alpha} + E(\epsilon_i|d_i = 1, Z_i)$ into its constituent components unless there is independent variation in $E(\epsilon_i|d_i = 1, Z_i)$ across observations, i.e., unless a regressor appears in equation (2). Without a regressor, $E(\epsilon_i|d_i = 1, Z_i)$ is a constant which cannot be distinguished from $\bar{\alpha}$.

This means that in models without regressors in the decision rule, we might as well work with the redefined model

$$Y_{it} = X_{it}\beta + d_i\alpha^* + \{U_{it} + d_i[\epsilon_i - E(\epsilon_i|d_i = 1)]\}, \tag{7}$$

where

$$\alpha^* = \bar{\alpha} + E(\epsilon_i | d_i = 1),$$

and content ourselves with the estimation of α^*. If everywhere we replace α with α^*, the fixed coefficient analysis of equation (1) applies to equation (7), provided that account is taken of the new error component in the disturbance when computing variances.

The parameter α^* answers question two. It addresses the question of determining the effect of training on the people selected as trainees. This parameter is useful in making forecasts when the same selection rule operates in the future that has operated in the past. In the presence of nonrandom selection into training, it does not answer question one. Indeed, without regressors in the decision rule of equation (2), question one cannot be answered, so far as we can see, unless specific distributional assumptions are invoked.

Random assignment of persons to training does not usually represent a relevant or interesting policy option. For this reason, we will focus attention on question two. Hence, if the training impact varies among individuals, we will seek to estimate α^* in equation (7). Since equation (7) may be reparametrized in the form of equation (1), we work exclusively with the fixed coefficient earnings function. Our earlier paper gives precise statements of conditions under which $\bar{\alpha}$ is identified in a random coefficient model (see Barros, 1986, for a more complete discussion).

Much of the statistical literature assumes that $\bar{\alpha}$ is the parameter of interest (see Fisher, 1953; Lee, 1978; Rosenbaum and Rubin 1983). In the context of estimating the impact of nonrandom treatments that are likely to be nonrandomly assigned in the future, $\bar{\alpha}$ is not an interesting policy or evaluation parameter since it does not recognize selection decisions by agents. Only if random assignment is to be followed in the future is there interest in this parameter. Of course, α^* is interesting for prediction purposes only to the extent that current selection rules will govern future participation. In this paper we do not address the more general problem of estimating future policy impacts when selection rules are changed. To answer this question requires stronger assumptions on the joint distribution of ϵ_i, U_{it}, and V_i than are required to estimate $\bar{\alpha}$ or α^*.

It is also important to note that any definition of the structural treatment coefficient is conditioned on the stability of the environment in which the program is operating. In the context of a training program, a tenfold expansion of training activity may affect the labor market for the trained and raise the cost of the training activity (and hence the content of programs). For either $\bar{\alpha}$ or α^* to be interesting parameters, it must be assumed that such effects are not present in the transition from the sample period to the future. If they are present, it is necessary to estimate how the change in the environment will affect these parameters. In this paper we abstract from these issues, as well as other possible sources of interdependence among outcomes. The resolution of these additional problems would require stronger assumptions than we have invoked here.[8]

Before concluding this section, it is important to note that there is a certain asymmetry in our analysis which, while natural in the context of models for the evaluation of the impact of training on earnings, may not be as natural in other contexts. In the context of a training program (and in the context of the analysis of schooling decisions), it is natural to reason in terms of a latent earnings function Y_{it}^* which exists in the absence of schooling or training options. "U_{it}" can be interpreted as latent ability or as skill useful in both trained and untrained occupations. Because of the natural temporal ordering of events, pretraining earnings is a natural concept and α_i is the markup (in dollar units) of skills due to participation in training. Note that nothing in this formulation restricts agents to have one or just two skills. Training can uncover or produce a new skill or enhance a single common skill. Parameter α^* is the gross return to training of the trained before the direct costs of training are subtracted.

In other contexts there is no natural temporal ordering of choices. In such cases the concept of α^* must be refined since there is no natural reference state. Corresponding to a definition of the gross gain using one state as a benchmark, there is a definition of gross gain using the other state as a benchmark. In the context of the Roy model [discussed following equation (6)], it is appropriate for an analysis of economic returns to outcomes to compute a gross gain for those who select sector 1 which compares *their* average earnings in sector 1 with what they would have earned on average in sector 0 and to compute a gross gain for those who select sector 0 which compares their average earnings in sector 0 with what they would have earned on average in sector 1.

To state this point more clearly, assume that X_{it} in the expression following equation (6) is a constant ($= 1$), and drop the time subscripts to reach the following simplified Roy model:

$$Y_{1i} = \mu_1 + U_{1i}$$
$$Y_{0i} = \mu_0 + U_{0i}.$$

In this notation,

$$\bar{\alpha} = \mu_1 - \mu_0$$
$$\epsilon_i = U_{1i} - U_{0i}.$$

The average gross gain for those who enter sector 1 from sector 0 is

$$\alpha_1^* = E(Y_{1i} - Y_{0i}|d_i = 1) = \bar{\alpha} + E(\epsilon_i|d_i = 1).$$

---

[8] This issue renders invalid use of estimates from the pilot negative income tax programs as estimates of the impact of a national negative income tax program. In the context of data from large-scale training programs, this issue is less cogent.

The average gross gain for those who enter sector 0 from sector 1 is

$$\alpha_0^* = E(Y_{0i} - Y_{1i}|d_i = 0) = -\bar{\alpha} - E(\epsilon_i|d_i = 0).$$

Both coefficients compare the average earnings in the outcome state and the average earnings in the alternative state for those who are in the outcome state. In a more general analysis, both α_1^* and α_0^* might be of interest. Provided that $\bar{\alpha}$ can be separated from $E(\epsilon_i|d_i = 1)$, α_0^* can be estimated exploiting the facts that $E(\epsilon_i) = 0$ and $E(d_i) = p$ are assumed to be known or estimable. No further identification conditions are required. For the sake of brevity and to focus on essential points, we do not develop this more general analysis here. The main point of this section—that $\bar{\alpha}$, the parameter of interest in statistical studies of selection bias, is not the parameter of behavioral interest—remains intact.

IV. Cross-Section Procedures

Standard cross-section procedures invoke unnecessarily strong assumptions. All that is required to identify α in a cross section is access to a regressor in equation (2). In the absence of a regressor, assumptions about the marginal distribution of U_{it} can be exploited to produce consistent estimators of the training impact.

A. Without Distributional Assumptions a Regressor Is Needed

Let $\bar{Y}_t^{(1)}$ denote the sample mean of trainee earnings and let $\bar{Y}_t^{(0)}$ denote the sample mean of nontrainee earnings:

$$\bar{Y}_t^{(1)} = \frac{\Sigma d_i Y_{it}}{\Sigma d_i}$$

$$\bar{Y}_t^{(0)} = \frac{\Sigma(1 - d_i) Y_{it}}{\Sigma(1 - d_i)},$$

assuming $0 < \Sigma d_i < I_t$, where I_t is the number of observations in period t. We retain the assumption that the data are generated by a random sampling scheme. If no regressors appear in equation (1), then $X_{it}\beta = \beta_t$ and

$$\text{plim } \bar{Y}_t^{(1)} = \beta_t + \alpha + E(U_{it}|d_i = 1)$$

$$\text{plim } \bar{Y}_t^{(0)} = \beta_t + E(U_{it}|d_i = 0).$$

Thus,

$$\text{plim}(\bar{Y}_t^{(1)} - \bar{Y}_t^{(0)}) = \alpha + \frac{E(U_{it}|d_i = 1)}{1 - p}$$

since $pE(U_{it}|d_i = 1) + (1 - p)E(U_{it}|d_i = 0) = 0$. Even if p were known, α cannot be separated from $E(U_{it}|d_i = 1)$ using cross-section data on sample means. Sample variances do not aid in securing identification unless $E(U_{it}^2|d_i = 0)$ or $E(U_{it}^2|d_i = 1)$ are known *a priori*. Similar remarks apply to the information available from higher moments unless they are restricted in some *a priori* fashion.

B. Overview of Cross-Section Procedures Which Use Regressors

If, however, $E(U_{it}|d_i = 1, Z_i)$ is a nonconstant function of Z_i, it is possible (with additional assumptions) to solve this identification problem. Securing identification in this fashion explicitly precludes a fully nonparametric strategy in which both the earnings function of equation (1) and decision rule of equation (2) are estimated in each (X_{it}, Z_i) stratum. For within each stratum, $E(U_{it}|d_i = 1, Z_i)$ is a constant function of Z_i and α is not identified from cross-section data. Restrictions across strata are required.

If $E(U_{it}|d_i = 1, Z_i)$ is a nonconstant function of Z_i, it is possible to exploit this information in a variety of ways depending on what else is assumed about the model. Here we simply sketch alternative strategies. In our earlier paper, we presented a systematic discussion of each approach.

(a) Suppose Z_i or a subset of Z_i is exogenous with respect to U_{it}. Under conditions specified more fully below, the exogenous subset may be used to construct an instrumental variable for d_i in equation (1), and α can be consistently estimated by instrumental variables methods. No explicit distributional assumptions about U_{it} or V_i are required (Heckman, 1978). The enrollment rule of equation (2) need not be fully specified.

(b) Suppose that Z_i is distributed independently of V_i and the functional form of the distribution of V_i is known. Under standard conditions, γ in equation (2) can be consistently estimated by conventional methods in discrete choice analysis (Amemiya, 1981). If Z_i is distributed independently of U_{it}, $F(-Z_i\hat{\gamma})$ can be used as an instrument for d_i in equation (1) (Heckman, 1978).

(c) Under the same conditions as specified in (b),

$$E(Y_{it}|X_{it}, Z_i) = X_{it}\beta + \alpha[1 - F(-Z_i\gamma)].$$

γ and α can be consistently estimated using $F(-Z_i\hat{\gamma})$ in place of $F(-Z_i\gamma)$ in the preceding equation (Heckman 1976, 1978) or else the preceding equation can be estimated by nonlinear least squares, estimating β, α and γ jointly (given the function form of F) (Barnow et al., 1980).

(d) If the functional forms of $E(U_{it}|d_i = 1, Z_i)$ and $E(U_{it}|d_i = 0, Z_i)$ as functions of Z_i are known up to a finite set of parameters, it is sometimes possible to consistently estimate β, α, and the parameters of the conditional means from the (nonlinear) regression function

$$
\begin{aligned}
E(Y_{it}|d_i, X_{it}, Z_i) = X_{it}\beta + d_i\alpha + d_i E(U_{it}|d_i = 1, Z_i) \\
+ (1 - d_i)E(U_{it}|d_i = 0, Z_i).
\end{aligned}
\tag{8}
$$

One way to acquire information about the functional form of $E(U_{it}|d_i = 1, Z_i)$ is to assume knowledge of the functional form of the joint distribution of (U_{it}, V_i) (e.g., that it is bivariate normal), but this is not required. Note further that this procedure does not require that Z_i be distributed independently of V_i in equation (2) (Heckman, 1980).

(e) Instead of (d), it is possible to do a two-stage estimation procedure if the joint density of (U_{it}, V_i) is assumed known up to a finite set of parameters and Z_i is distributed independently of V_i and U_{it}. In stage one, $E(U_{it}|d_i = 1, Z_i)$ and $E(U_{it}|d_i = 0, Z_i)$ are determined up to some unknown parameters by conventional discrete choice analysis. Then the regression of equation (8) is run using estimated E values in place of population E values on the right hand side of the equation (Heckman, 1976). In Section X we establish the relationship between this procedure and the propensity score method of Rosenbaum and Rubin (1983).

(f) Under the assumptions of (e), use maximum likelihood to consistently estimate α (Heckman, 1978).

Note that a separate value of α may be estimated for each cross section, so that depending on the number of cross sections it is possible to estimate growth and decay effects in training (i.e., α_t can be estimated for each cross section).

Conventional selection bias approaches (d), (e), and (f) as well as (b) and (c) rely on strong distributional assumptions or else assumptions about nonlinearities in the model, but in fact these are not required. Distributional assumptions are usually not motivated by behavioral theory. Given that a regressor appears in the decision rule of equation (2), if it is uncorrelated with U_{it}, the regressor is an instrumental variable for d_i. It is not necessary to invoke strong distributional assumptions, but if they are invoked, Z_i need not be uncorrelated with U_{it}. In many papers, however, Z_i and U_{it} are usually assumed to be independent. The imposition of overidentifying "information," if false, may lead to considerable bias and instability in the estimates. However, the overidentifying assumptions are testable, and so such false restrictions need not be imposed. Conventional practice imposes these overidentifying restrictions without testing them. We next discuss the instrumental variables procedure in greater detail.[9]

---

[9] Notice that in a transition from a fixed coefficient model to a random coefficient model the analysis of this section focuses on estimation of α^* for the latter. Clearly, U_{it} in equation (7), is redefined to include $d_i[\epsilon_i - E(\epsilon_i|d_i = 1)]$. With this modification, all of our analysis in the text remains intact.

C. The Instrumental Variable Estimator

This estimator is the least demanding in the *a priori* conditions that must be satisfied for its use. It requires the following assumptions:

(a) There is at least one variable in $Z_i,(Z_i^e)$ with a nonzero γ coefficient in equation (2), such that for some known transfor-   (9a)
mation of $Z_i^e,[g(Z_i^e)]$, $E[U_{it}g(Z_i^e)] = 0$.
(b) Array X_{it} and d_i into a vector $J_{1it} = (X_{it}, d_i)$. Array X_{it} and $g(Z_i^e)$ into a vector $J_{2it} = [X_{it}, g(Z_i^e)]$. In this notation, it is assumed that

$$E\left(\sum_{i=1}^{I_t} \frac{J_{2it}'J_{1it}}{I_t} \right) \tag{9b}$$

has full column rank uniformly in I_t for I_t sufficiently large where I_t denotes the number of individuals in period t.

With these assumptions, the instrumental variable (IV) estimator

$$\begin{bmatrix} \hat{\beta} \\ \hat{\alpha} \end{bmatrix}_{\text{IV}} = \left(\sum_{i=1}^{I_t} \frac{J_{2it}'J_{1it}}{I_t} \right)^{-1} \sum_{i=1}^{I_t} \frac{J_{2it}'Y_{it}}{I_t}$$

is consistent for (β, α) regardless of any covariance between U_{it} and d_i.

It is important to notice how weak these conditions are. The functional form of the distribution of V_i need not be known. Z_i need not be distributed independently of V_i. Moreover, $g(Z_i^e)$ may be a nonlinear function of variables appearing in X_{it} as long as conditions 9(a) and 9(b) are satisfied.

The instrumental variable $g(Z_i^e)$ may also be a lagged value of time-varying variables appearing in X_{it}, provided the analyst has access to longitudinal data. The rank condition (9b) will generally be satisfied in this case as long as X_{it} exhibits serial dependence. Thus, longitudinal data (on exogenous characteristics) may provide a source of instrumental variables.

D. Identification Through Distributional Assumptions About the Marginal Distribution of U_{it}

If no regressor appears in the decision rule of equation (2), the estimators presented so far in this section cannot be used to consistently estimate α. Heckman (1978) demonstrates that if (U_{it}, V_i) are normally distributed, α is identified even if there is no regressor in equation (2). His conditions are overly strong.

If U_{it} has zero third and fifth central moments, α is identified even if no regressor appears in the enrollment rule. This assumption about U_{it} is implied by normality or symmetry of the density of U_{it}, but it is weaker than either provided that the required moments are finite. The fact that α can be identified by invoking distributional assumptions about U_{it} illustrates the more general point that there is a tradeoff between assumptions about regressors and assumptions about the distribution of U_{it} that must be invoked to identify α.

We have established that under the following assumptions, α in equation (1) is identified:

$$\text{(a)} \quad E(U_{it}^3) = 0$$

$$\text{(b)} \quad E(U_{it}^5) = 0 \tag{10}$$

$$\text{(c)} \quad (U_{it}, V_i) \quad \text{is iid.}$$

A consistent method-of-moments estimator can be devised that exploits these assumptions (see Heckman and Robb, 1985). Find $\hat{\alpha}$ that sets a weighted average of the sample analogs of $E(U_{it}^3)$ and $E(U_{it}^5)$ as close to zero as possible.

To simplify the exposition, suppose that there are no regressors in the earnings function of equation (1), so $X_{it}\beta = \beta_t$. The proposed estimator finds the value of $\hat{\alpha}$ that sets

$$\frac{1}{I_t} \sum_{i=1}^{I_t} \left[(Y_{it} - \overline{Y}_t) - \bar{\alpha}(d_i - \bar{d}) \right]^3 \tag{11a}$$

and

$$\frac{1}{I_t} \sum_{i=1}^{I_t} \left[(Y_{it} - \overline{Y}_t) - \hat{\alpha}(d_i - \bar{d}) \right]^5 \tag{11b}$$

as close to zero as possible in a suitably chosen metric where as before, an overbar denotes sample mean. A pair of moments is required in order to pick the unique consistent root. In our companion paper, we establish the existence of a unique root that sets expressions (11a) and (11b) to zero in large samples. Obviously other moment restrictions could be used to identify α.[10]

---

[10] The remark in footnote 9 applies with full force in this section. Different assumptions are being made in the case of estimating α^* than are invoked in the case of estimating the fixed coefficient model, i.e., third and fifth moment assumptions are being invoked about $U_{it} + d_i[\epsilon_i - E(\epsilon_i | d_i = 1)]$ in the former case. The main point—that if *some* moment assumptions are being invoked it is possible to estimate α or α^*—remains intact.

E. Selection on Observables

In the special case in which

$$E(U_{it}|d_i, Z_i) = E(U_{it}|Z_i),$$

selection is said to occur on the observables. Such a case can arise if U_{it} is distributed independently of V_i in equation (2), but U_{it} and Z_i are stochastically dependent (i.e., some of the observables in the enrollment equation are correlated with the unobservables in the earnings equation). In this case U_{it} and d_i can be shown to be conditionally independent given Z_i. If it is further assumed that U_{it} and V_i conditional on Z_i are independent, then U_{it} and d_i can be shown to be conditionally independent given Z_i. In the notation of Dawid (1979) as used by Rosenbaum and Rubin (1983),

$$U_{it} \perp\!\!\!\perp d_i | Z_i,$$

i.e., given Z_i, d_i is strongly ignorable. In a random coefficient model the required condition is

$$(U_{it} + \epsilon_i d_i) \perp\!\!\!\perp d_i | Z_i.$$

The strategy for consistent estimation presented in Section B must be modified; in particular, methods (a)–(c) are inappropriate. However, method (d) still applies and simplifies because

$$E(U_{it}|d_i = 1, Z_i) = E(U_{it}|d_i = 0, Z_i) = E(U_{it}|Z_i),$$

so that we obtain in place of equation (8)

$$E(Y_{it}|d_i, Y_{it}, Z_i) = X_{it}\beta + d_i\alpha + E(U_{it}|Z_i). \tag{8'}$$

Specifying the joint distribution of (U_{it}, Z_i) or just the conditional mean of U_{it} given Z_i, produces a formula for $E(U_{it}|Z_i)$ up to a set of parameters. The model can be estimated by nonlinear regression. Conditions for the existence of a consistent estimator of α are presented in our companion paper (see also Barnow et al., 1980).

Method (e) of Section B no longer directly applies. Except in unusual circumstances (e.g., a single element in Z_i), there is no relationship between any of the parameters of $E(U_{it}|Z_i)$ and the propensity score $\Pr(d_i = 1|Z_i)$, so that conventional two-stage estimators generated from discrete choice theory do not produce useful information. Method (f) produces a consistent estimator provided that an explicit probabilistic relationship between U_{it} and Z_i is postulated.[11]

---

[11] The remarks made in footnotes 9 and 10 apply in this section as well.

F. Summary

Conventional cross-section practice invokes numerous extraneous assumptions to secure identification of α. These overidentifying restrictions are rarely tested, although they are testable. Strong distributional assumptions are not required to estimate α. Assumptions about the distributions of unobservables are rarely justified by an appeal to behavioral theory. Assumptions about the presence of regressors in enrollment equations and assumptions about stochastic dependence relationships among U_{it}, Z_i, and d_i are sometimes justified by behavioral theory.

V. Repeated Cross-Section Methods for the Case When Training Identity of Individuals Is Unknown

In a time homogeneous environment, estimates of the population mean earnings formed in two or more cross sections of unrelated persons can be used to obtain selection-bias-free estimates of the training effect even if the training status of each person is unknown (but the population proportion of trainees is known or can be consistently estimated). With more data, the time homogeneity assumption can be partially relaxed.

Assuming a time homogeneous environment and access to repeated cross-section data and random sampling, it is possible to identify α (a) without any regressor in the decision rule, (b) without need to specify the joint distribution of U_{it} and V_i, and (c) without any need to know which individuals in the sample enrolled in training (but the proportion of trainees must be known or consistently estimable).

To see why this claim is true, suppose that no regressors appear in the earnings function.[12] In the notation of equation (1), $X_{it}\beta = \beta_t$. Then, assuming that a random sampling scheme generates the data,

$$\text{plim } \overline{Y}_t = \text{plim} \frac{\Sigma Y_{it}}{I_t} = E(\beta_t + \alpha d_i + U_{it}) = \beta_t + \alpha p \qquad t > k$$

$$\text{plim } \overline{Y}_{t'} = \text{plim} \frac{\Sigma Y_{it'}}{I_{t'}} = E(\beta_{t'} + U_{it'}) = \beta_{t'} \qquad t' < k.$$

---

[12] If regressors appear in the earnings functions, the following procedure can be used. Rewrite equation (1) as $Y_{it} = \beta_t + X_{it}\pi + d_i\alpha + U_{it}$. It is possible to estimate π from preprogram data. (This assumes there are no time invariant variables in X_{it}. If there are such variables, they may be deleted from the regressor vector and π appropriately redefined without affecting the analysis.) Replace Y_{it} by $Y_{it} - X_{it}\hat{\pi}$ and the analysis in the text goes through. Note that we are assuming that no X_{it} variables become nonconstant after period k.

In a time homogeneous environment, $\beta_t = \beta_{t'}$ and

$$\text{plim} \frac{\overline{Y}_t - \overline{Y}_{t'}}{\hat{p}} = \alpha,$$

where $\hat{p}$ is a consistent estimator of $p = E(d_i)$.

With more than two years of repeated cross-section data, one can apply the same principles to identify α while relaxing the time homogeneity assumption. For instance, suppose that population mean earnings lie on a polynomial of order $L - 2$:

$$\beta_t = \pi_0 + \pi_1 t + \cdots + \pi_{L-2} t^{L-2}.$$

From L temporally distinct cross sections, it is possible to estimate consistently the $L - 1$ π-parameters and α provided that the number of observations in each cross section becomes large and there is at least one preprogram and one postprogram cross section.

If the effect of training differs across periods, it is still possible to identify α_t provided that the environment changes in a "sufficiently regular" way. For example, suppose

$$\beta_t = \pi_0 + \pi_1 t$$

$$\alpha_t = \phi_0 (\phi_1)^{t-k} \qquad t > k.$$

In this case, π_0, π_1, ϕ_0, and ϕ_1 are identified from the means of four cross sections, as long as at least two of these means come from a preprogram period and two come from successive postprogram periods.

In our companion paper we state more rigorously the conditions required to consistently estimate α using repeated cross-section data which do not record the training identity of individuals. Section IX examines the sensitivity of this class of estimators to violations of the random sampling assumption.

VI. Longitudinal Procedures

Most longitudinal procedures require knowledge of certain moments of the joint distribution of unobservables in the earnings and enrollment equations. We present several illustrations of this claim, as well as a counterexample. The counterexample identifies α by assuming only that the error term in the earnings equation is covariance stationary.

We now consider four examples of estimators which use longitudinal data.

A. The Fixed Effects Method

This method was developed by Mundlak (1961, 1978) and refined by Chamberlain (1982). It is widely used in recent social science data analyses.

It is based on the following assumption:

$$E(U_{it} - U_{it'}|d_i, X_{it} - X_{it'}) = 0 \qquad \text{for all } t, t', t > k > t'. \qquad (12)$$

As a consequence of this assumption, we may write a difference regression as

$$E(Y_{it} - Y_{it'}|X_{it} - X_{it'}, d_i) = (X_{it} - X_{it'})\beta + d_i\alpha \qquad t > k > t'.$$

Suppose that condition (12) holds and the analyst has access to one year of preprogram and one year of postprogram earnings. Regressing the difference between postprogram earnings in any year and earnings in any preprogram year on the change in regressors between those years and a dummy variable for training status produces a consistent estimator of α.

Some decision rules and error processes for earnings produce condition (12). For example, consider a certainty environment in which the earnings residual has a permanent-transitory structure:

$$U_{it} = \phi_i + \epsilon_{it} \qquad (13)$$

where ϵ_{it} is a mean zero random variable independent of all other values of $\epsilon_{it'}$ for $t \neq t'$ and is distributed independently of ϕ_i, a mean zero person-specific time-invariant random variable. Assuming that S_i in the decision rule of equation (5) is distributed independently of all ϵ_{it} except possibly for ϵ_{ik}, then condition (12) will be satisfied. With two periods of data (in t and t', $t > k > t'$) α is just identified. With more periods of panel data, the model is overidentified and hence condition (12) is subject to test (Chamberlain, 1982).

Condition (12) may also be satisfied in an environment of uncertainty. Suppose equation (13) governs the error structure in equation (1) and

$$E_{k-1}(\epsilon_{ik}) = 0,$$

but

$$E_{k-1}(\phi_i) = \phi_i$$

so that agents cannot forecast innovations in their earnings but they know their own permanent component. Provided that S_i is distributed independently of all ϵ_{it} except possibly for ϵ_{ik}, this model also produces condition (12).

We investigate the plausibility of condition (12) with respect to more general decision rules and error processes in Section VIII.[13]

B. U_{it} Follows a First-Order Autoregressive Process

Suppose next that U_{it} follows a first-order autoregression:

$$U_{it} = \rho U_{i,t-1} + \nu_{it} \qquad (14)$$

---

[13] We repeat the point made in footnotes 9, 10, and 11 that if α^* is the coefficient of interest, U_{it} is redefined to be $U_{it} + d_i[\epsilon_i - E(\epsilon_i|d_i = 1)]$.

where $E(\nu_{it}) = 0$ and the ν_{it} are mutually independently (not necessarily identically) distributed random variables with $\rho \neq 1$. Substitution using equations (1) and (14) to solve for U_{it} yields

$$Y_{it} = \left[X_{it} - \left(X_{it'}\rho^{t-t'} \right) \right]\beta + \left(1 - \rho^{t-t'} \right)d_i\alpha$$

$$+ \rho^{t-t'}Y_{it'} + \left\{ \sum_{j=0}^{t-(t'+1)} \rho^j\nu_{i,\,t-j} \right\} \qquad t > t' > k. \qquad (15)$$

Assume further that the perfect foresight rule of equation (5) determines enrollment and that the ν_{ij} are distributed independently of S_i and X_{ik} in equation (5). Heckman and Wolpin (1976) invoke similar assumptions in their analysis of affirmative action programs. If X_{ij} is independent of $\nu_{ij'}$ for all j, j' (an overly strong condition) then (linear or nonlinear) least squares applied to equation (15) consistently estimates α as the number of observations becomes large. (The appropriate nonlinear regression increases efficiency by imposing the implied cross coefficient restrictions.) As is the case with the fixed effect estimator, increasing the length of the panel and keeping the same assumptions, the model becomes overidentified (and hence testable) for panels with more than two observations.[14]

C. U_{it} Is Covariance Stationary

The next procedure invokes an assumption implicitly used in many papers on training (e.g., Ashenfelter, 1978; Bassi, 1983), but exploits the assumption in a novel way. We assume

(a) U_{it} is covariance stationary so $E(U_{it}U_{i,\,t-j}) = \sigma_j$ for $j \geq 0$;
(b) access to at least two observations on preprogram earnings in t' and $t' - j$ as well as one observation on postprogram earnings   (16) in t where $t - t' = j$; and
(c) $pE(U_{it'}|d_i = 1) \neq 0$.

Unlike the two previous examples, we make no assumptions here about the

---

[14] In the context of estimating α^* in the random coefficient model, it is not natural to specify equation (14) in the text for the redefined U_{it}. In general if U_{it} has an autoregressive representation, $U_{it} + d_i[\epsilon_i - E(\epsilon_i|d_i = 1)]$ will not. A more natural specification models error component $d_i[\epsilon_i - E(\epsilon_i|d_i = 1)]$ as a permanent postprogram component in the error term. In place of the error term in braces in Equation (15), write

$$\sum_{j=0}^{t-(t'+1)} \rho^j\nu_{i,\,t-j} + \phi_i\left(1 - \rho^{t-t'} \right) \qquad t, t' > k$$

where $\phi_i = d_i[\epsilon_i - E(\epsilon_i|d_i = 1)]$. Orthogonality conditions will *not* be satisfied between ϕ_i and $Y_{it'}$, and an instrument for lagged $Y_{it'}$ will be required to consistently estimate α^* or else the time series methods of MaCurdy (1982) will have to be invoked to obtain consistent estimators.

appropriate enrollment rule or about the stochastic relationship between U_{it} and the cost of enrollment S_i.

By the argument of footnote 12, we lose no generality by suppressing the effect of regressors in equation (1). Thus let

$$Y_{it} = \beta_t + d_i\alpha + U_{it} \qquad t > k$$
$$Y_{it'} = \beta_{t'} + U_{it'} \qquad t' < k,$$

where β_t and $\beta_{t'}$ are period-specific shifters.

From a random sample of preprogram earnings from periods t' and $t' - j$, σ_j can be consistently estimated from the sample covariances between $Y_{it'}$ and $Y_{i,t'-j}$:

$$m_1 = \frac{\Sigma\left[(Y_{it'} - \overline{Y}_{t'})(Y_{i,t'-j} - \overline{Y}_{t'-j})\right]}{I_t}$$

$$\text{plim } m_1 = \sigma_j.$$

If $t > k$ and $t - t' = j$ so that the postprogram earnings data are as far removed in time from t' as t' is removed from $t' - j$, form the sample covariance between Y_{it} and $Y_{it'}$:

$$m_2 = \frac{\Sigma\left[(Y_{it} - \overline{Y}_t)(Y_{it'} - \overline{Y}_{t'})\right]}{I_t},$$

which has the probability limit

$$\text{plim } m_2 = \sigma_j + \alpha pE(U_{it'}|d_i = 1) \qquad t > k > t'.$$

From the sample covariance between d_i and $Y_{it'}$,

$$m_3 = \frac{\Sigma\left[(Y_{it'} - \overline{Y}_{t'})d_i\right]}{I_t}$$

with probability limit

$$\text{plim } m_3 = pE(U_{it'}|d_i = 1) \qquad t' < k.$$

Combining this information and assuming $pE(U_{it'}|d_i = 1) \neq 0$ for $t' < k$,

$$\text{plim } \hat{\alpha} = \text{plim } \frac{m_2 - m_1}{m_3} = \alpha.$$

For panels of sufficient length (e.g., more than two preprogram observations or more than two postprogram observations), the stationarity assumption can be tested. Thus as before, increasing the length of the panel converts a just identified model to an overidentified one.[15]

---

[15]As in footnotes 9, 10, and 11, we emphasize that different assumptions are being made in the random coefficient version of the model than are made in the fixed coefficient version. Note, however, that in this section we do not require that variances be equal in preprogram and postprogram periods so that the estimator $\hat{\alpha}$ is still appropriate as an estimator for α^* if, e.g., U_{it} is uncorrelated with $d_i[\epsilon_i - E(\epsilon_i|d_i = 1)]$ for all t.

D. An Unrestricted Process for U_{it} When Agents Do Not Know Future Innovations in Their Earnings

The estimator proposed in this subsection assumes that agents cannot perfectly predict future earnings. More specifically, for an agent whose relevant earnings history begins N periods before period k, we assume that

(a) $$E_{k-1}(U_{ik}) = E(U_{ik}|U_{i,k-1}, \ldots, U_{i,k-N}),$$

i.e., that predictions of future U_{it} are made solely on the basis of previous values of U_{it}. Past values of the exogenous variables are assumed to have no predictive value for U_{ik}.

In addition, we assume that

(b) the relevant earnings history goes back N periods before period k;
(c) the enrollment decision is characterized by equation (4);
(d) S_i and X_{ik} are known as of period $k-1$ when the enrollment decision is being made;
(e) X_{it} is distributed independently of U_{ij} for all t and j; and
(f) S_i is distributed independently of U_{ij} for all j.

Defining

$$\psi_i = (Y_{i,k-1} - X_{i,k-1}\beta, \ldots, Y_{i,k-N} - X_{i,k-N}\beta)$$

and

$$G(\psi_i) = E(d_i|\psi_i),$$

under the conditions given above, α can be consistently estimated. We define

$$p = E(d_i),$$

and

$$c = \frac{E[U_{it}(G(\psi_i) - p)]}{E(G(\psi_i) - p)^2}.$$

We rewrite equation (1) in the following way:

$$Y_{it} = X_{it}\beta + d_i\alpha + c(G(\psi_i) - p) + [U_{it} - c(G(\psi_i) - p)]. \tag{17}$$

This defines an estimating equation for the parameters of the model. In the transformed equation

$$E\{X_{it}'[U_{it} - c(G(\psi_i) - p)]\} = 0$$

by assumption (e) above. The transformed residual is uncorrelated with $c(G(\psi_i) - p)$ from the definition of c.

Thus, it remains to show that

$$E\{d_i[U_{it} - c(G(\psi_i) - p)]\} = 0.$$

Before proving this it is helpful to notice that as a consequence of assumptions (a), (d), and (e),

$$E(d_i|U_{it}, U_{i,t-1}, \ldots, U_{i,k-1}, \ldots, U_{i,k-N})$$
$$= E(d_i|U_{i,k-1}, \ldots, U_{i,k-N}) \qquad t > k. \tag{18}$$

This relationship is proved in our companion paper. Since only preprogram innovations determine participation and because U_{it} is distributed independently of X_{ik} and S_i in the decision rule of equation (4), the conditional mean of d_i does not depend on postprogram values of U_{it} given all preprogram values.

Intuitively, the term $U_{it} - c(G(\psi_i) - p)$ is orthogonal to $G(\psi_i)$, the best predictor of d_i based on ψ_i; if $U_{it} - c(G(\psi_i) - p)$ were correlated with d_i, it would mean that U_{it} helped to predict d_i, contradicting condition (18).

The proof of the proposition uses the fact from condition (18) that $E(d_i|\psi_i, U_{it}) = G(\psi_i)$ in computing the expectation

$$E\{d_i[U_{it} - c(G(\psi_i) - p)]\}$$
$$= E[E\{d_i[U_{it} - c(G(\psi_i) - p)]\}|\psi_i, U_{it}]$$
$$= E\{[U_{it} - c(G(\psi_i) - p)]E(d_i|\psi_i, U_{it})\}$$
$$= E\{[U_{it} - c(G(\psi_i) - p)]G(\psi_i)\}$$
$$= 0$$

as a consequence of the definition of c.

The elements of ψ_i can be consistently estimated by fitting a preprogram earnings equation and forming the residuals from preprogram earnings data to estimate $U_{i,k-1}, \ldots, U_{k,k-N}$. One can assume a functional form for G and estimate the parameters of G using standard methods in discrete choice applied to enrollment data.[16]

VII. Repeated Cross-Section Analogs of Longitudinal Procedures

Most longitudinal procedures can be fit on repeated cross-section data. Repeated cross-section data are cheaper to collect, and they do not suffer from problems of nonrandom attrition which plague panel data.

The previous section presented longitudinal estimators of α. In all cases but one, however, α can actually be identified with repeated cross-section data. Here we establish this claim. Our earlier paper gives additional

---

[16] In the context of estimating α^* the estimator of this section requires that predictions of future $U_{it} + d_i[\epsilon_i - E(\epsilon_i|d_i = 1)]$ are based solely on preprogram values of U_{it} ($t < k$).

examples of longitudinal estimators which can be implemented on repeated cross-section data. We have been unable to produce a repeated cross-section estimator of the method given in Section VID.

A. The Fixed Effect Model

As in Section VIA, assume that condition (12) holds so

$$E(U_{it}|d_i = 1) = E(U_{it'}|d_i = 1)$$

$$E(U_{it}|d_i = 0) = E(U_{it'}|d_i = 0) \qquad t > k > t'$$

for all t, t'. Let $X_{it}\beta = \beta_t$ and define $\hat{\alpha}$ in terms of the notation of Section IVA

$$\hat{\alpha} = \left(\overline{Y}_t^{(1)} - \overline{Y}_t^{(0)}\right) - \left(\overline{Y}_{t'}^{(1)} - \overline{Y}_{t'}^{(0)}\right).$$

Assuming random sampling, consistency of $\hat{\alpha}$ follows immediately from condition (12):

$$\begin{aligned}
\text{plim } \alpha &= \left[\alpha + \beta_t - \beta_{t'} + E(U_{it}|d_i = 1) - E(U_{it}|d_i = 0)\right] \\
&\quad - \left[\beta_t - \beta_{t'} + E(U_{it'}|d_i = 1) - E(U_{it'}|d_i = 0)\right] \\
&= \alpha.
\end{aligned}$$

As in the case of the longitudinal version of this estimator, with more than two cross sections, the hypothesis of condition (12) is subject to test (i.e., the model is overidentified).

B. U_{it} Follows a First-Order Autoregressive Process

In one respect the preceding example is contrived. It assumes that in preprogram cross sections we know the identity of future trainees. Such data might exist (e.g., individuals in the training period k might be asked about their preperiod k earnings to see if they qualify for admission), but this seems unlikely. One advantage of longitudinal data for estimating α in the fixed effect model is that if the survey extends before period k, the identity of future trainees is known.

The need for preprogram earnings to identify α is, however, only an artifact of the fixed-effect assumption of equation (13). Suppose instead that U_{it} follows a first-order autoregressive process given by equation (14) and that

$$E(\nu_{it}|d_i) = 0 \qquad t > k \qquad (19)$$

as in Section VIB. With three successive postprogram cross sections in which the identity of trainees is known, it is possible to identify α.

To establish this result, let the three postprogram periods be t, $t+1$ and $t+2$. Assuming, as before, that no regressor appears in equation (1),

$$\text{plim } \overline{Y}_j^{(1)} = \beta_j + \alpha + E\left(U_{ij}|d_i = 1\right)$$

$$\text{plim } \overline{Y}_j^{(0)} = \beta_j + E\left(U_{ij}|d_i = 0\right).$$

From condition (19),

$$E\left(U_{i,t+1}|d_i = 1\right) = \rho E\left(U_{it}|d_i = 1\right)$$

$$E\left(U_{i,t+1}|d_i = 0\right) = \rho E\left(U_{it}|d_i = 0\right)$$

$$E\left(U_{i,t+2}|d_i = 1\right) = \rho^2 E\left(U_{it}|d_i = 1\right)$$

$$E\left(U_{i,t+2}|d_i = 0\right) = \rho^2 E\left(U_{it}|d_i = 0\right).$$

Using these formulae, it is straightforward to verify that $\hat{\rho}$ defined by

$$\hat{\rho} = \frac{\left(\overline{Y}_{t+2}^{(1)} - \overline{Y}_{t+2}^{(0)}\right) - \left(\overline{Y}_{t+1}^{(1)} - \overline{Y}_{t+1}^{(0)}\right)}{\left(\overline{Y}_{t+1}^{(1)} - \overline{Y}_{t+1}^{(0)}\right) - \left(\overline{Y}_{t}^{(1)} - \overline{Y}_{t}^{(0)}\right)}$$

is consistent for ρ and that $\hat{\alpha}$ defined by

$$\hat{\alpha} = \frac{\left(\overline{Y}_{t+2}^{(1)} - \overline{Y}_{t+2}^{(0)}\right) - \hat{\rho}\left(\overline{Y}_{t+1}^{(1)} - \overline{Y}_{t+1}^{(0)}\right)}{1 - \hat{\rho}}$$

is consistent for α.[17]

For this model, the advantage of longitudinal data is clear. Only two time periods of longitudinal data are required to identify α, but three periods of repeated cross-section data are required to estimate the same parameter. However, if Y_{it} is subject to measurement error, the apparent advantages of longitudinal data become less clear. Repeated cross-section estimators are robust to mean zero measurement error in the variables. The longitudinal regression estimator discussed in Section VIB does not identify α unless the analyst observes earnings without error. Given three years of longitudinal data and assuming that measurement error is serially uncorrelated, one could instrument Y_{it}, in equation (15), using earnings in the earliest year as an instrument. This requires one more year of data. Thus one advantage of the longitudinal estimator disappears in the presence of measurement error.[18] With four or more repeated cross sections, the model is obviously overidentified and hence subject to test.

---

[17] This estimator is obviously consistent for either the fixed coefficient (α) or random coefficient (α^*) model since $E\{d_i[\epsilon_i - E(\epsilon_i|d_i = 1)]|d_i = 1\} = 0$.

[18] Recall from our discussion in footnote 14 that in the random coefficient model developed there an instrument for $Y_{it'}$ is required even in the absence of measurement error.

C. Covariance Stationarity

For simplicity we assume that there are no regressors in the earnings equation and let $X_{it}\beta = \beta_t$ (see Heckman and Robb, 1985, for the case in which regressors are present). Assume that conditions (16) are satisfied. Before presenting the repeated cross section estimator, it is helpful to record the following facts:

$$\text{Var}(Y_{it}) = \alpha^2(1-p)p + 2\alpha E(U_{it}|d_i=1)p + \sigma_u^2 \qquad t > k \quad (20a)$$

$$\text{Var}(Y_{it'}) = \sigma_u^2 \qquad t' < k \qquad (20b)$$

$$\text{Cov}(Y_{it}, d_i) = \alpha p(1-p) + pE(U_{it}|d_i=1). \qquad (20c)$$

Note that $E(U_{it}^2) = E(U_{it'}^2)$ by virtue of assumption (16a). Then

$$\hat{\alpha} = [p(1-p)]^{-1}\left[\left[\frac{\sum(Y_{it}-\bar{Y}_t)d_i}{I_t}\right.\right.$$

$$-\left\{\left[\frac{\sum(Y_{it}-\bar{Y}_t)d_i}{I_t}\right]^2\right. \qquad (21)$$

$$\left.\left.\left. -p(1-p)\left[\frac{\sum(Y_{it}-\bar{Y}_t)^2}{I_t} - \frac{\sum(Y_{it'}-\bar{Y}_{t'})^2}{I_{t'}}\right]\right\}^{1/2}\right]\right]$$

is consistent for α.

This expression arises by subtracting equation (20b) from (20a). Then use equation (20c) to get an expression for $E(U_{it}|d_i=1)$ which can be substituted into the expression for the difference between equation (20a) and (20b). Replacing population moments by sample counterparts produces a quadratic equation in $\hat{\alpha}$, with the negative root given by equation (21). The positive root is inconsistent for α.[19]

Notice that the estimators of Sections VIC and VIIC exploit different features of the covariance stationarity assumptions. The longitudinal procedure only requires that $E(U_{it}U_{i,t-j}) = E(U_{it'} U_{i,t'-j})$ for $j > 0$; variances need not be equal across periods. The repeated cross section analog above only requires that $E(U_{it}U_{i,t-j}) = E(U_{it'} U_{i,t'-j})$ for $j = 0$; covariances may

---

[19] This estimator requires that the variance of U_{it} ($t > k$) be the same as the variance of $U_{it'}$ ($t' < k$). Thus, in the random coefficient model, if U_{it} has a constant variance, $U_{it} + d_i[\epsilon_i - E(\epsilon_i|d_i=1)]$ will not have the same variance as $U_{it'}$. It is possible, but artificial, to invoke equality of the variances for the two disturbance terms. Thus, in this sense our proposed covariance stationary estimator is *not* robust when applied to estimate α^* in repeated cross-section data.

differ among equispaced pairs of the U_{it}. With more than two cross sections, the covariance stationarity assumption is overidentifying and hence subject to test.

VIII. First Difference or Fixed Effect Methods

Plausible economic models do not justify first difference methods. Lessons drawn from these methods are misleading.

A. Models which Justify Condition (12)

Whenever condition (12) holds, α can be estimated consistently from the difference regression method described in Section VIA. This section presents a model which satisfies condition (12): the earnings residual has a permanent-transitory structure, the decision rules of equations (4) or (5) determine enrollment, and S_i is distributed independently of the transitory component of U_{it}.

However, this model is rather special. It is very easy to produce plausible models that do not satisfy condition (12). For example, even if equation (13) characterizes U_{it}, if S_i in equation (5) does not have the same joint (bivariate) distribution with respect to all ϵ_{it}, except for ϵ_{ik}, condition (12) may be violated.

Even if S_i in equation (5) is distributed independently of U_{it} for all t, it is still not the case that condition (12) is satisfied in a general model. For example, suppose X_{it} is distributed independently of all U_{it} and let

$$U_{it} = \rho U_{i,t-1} + \nu_{it},$$

where ν_{it} is a mean zero, iid random variable and $|\rho| < 1$. If $\rho \neq 0$ and the perfect foresight decision rule characterizes enrollment, condition (12) is not satisfied for $t > k > t'$ because

$$E(U_{it}|d_i = 1) = E(U_{it}|U_{ik} + X_{ik}\beta - \alpha/r < S_i)$$

$$= \rho^{t-k}E(U_{ik}|d_i = 1)$$

$$\neq E(U_{it'}|d_i = 1) = E(U_{it'}|U_{ik} + X_{ik}\beta - \alpha/r < S_i)$$

unless the conditional expectations are linear (in U_{ik}) for all t and $k - t' = t - k$. In that case

$$E(U_{it'}|d_i = 1) = \rho^{k-t'}E(U_{ik}|d_i = 1),$$

so $E(U_{it} - U_{it'}|d_i = 1) = 0$ only for t, t' such that $k - t' = t - k$. Thus, condition (12) is not satisfied for all $t > k > t'$.

For more general specifications of U_{it} and stochastic dependence between S_i and U_{it}, condition (12) will not be satisfied.

B. More General First Difference Estimators

Instead of condition (12), assume that

$$E[(U_{it} - U_{it'})(X_{it} - X_{it'})] = 0 \qquad \text{for some} \quad t, t', t > k > t'$$
$$E[(U_{it} - U_{it'})d_i] = 0 \qquad \text{for some} \quad t > k > t'. \tag{22}$$

Two new ideas are embodied in this assumption. In place of the assumption that $U_{it} - U_{it'}$ be conditionally independent of $X_{it} - X_{it'}$ and d_i, we only require uncorrelatedness. Also, rather than assume that $E(U_{it} - U_{it'}|d_i, X_{it} - X_{it'}) = 0$ for all $t > k > t'$, the correlation needs to be zero only for some $t > k > t'$. For the appropriate values of t and t', least squares applied to the differenced data consistently estimates α.

Our companion paper presents three examples of models that satisfy condition (22) but not (12). Here we discuss one of them.

Suppose that

(a) U_{it} is covariance stationary;
(b) U_{it} has a linear regression on U_{ik} for all t (i.e., $E(U_{it}|U_{ik}) = \beta_{tk}U_{ik}$);
(c) the U_{it} are mutually independent of (X_{ik}, S_i) for all t;
(d) α is common to all individuals (so the model is of the fixed $\qquad$ (23)
      coefficient form); and
(e) the environment is one of perfect foresight where the decision
      rule of equation (5) determines participation.

Under these assumptions, condition (22) is satisfied.

To see this, note that (a) and (b) above imply that there exists a δ such that

$$U_{it} = U_{i,k+j} = \delta U_{ik} + \omega_{it} \qquad j > 0, t = k + j$$
$$U_{it'} = U_{i,k-j} = \delta U_{ik} + \omega_{it'} \qquad j > 0, t' = k - j$$

for *some* $j > 0$, and

$$E(\omega_{it}|U_{ik}) = E(\omega_{it'}|U_{ik}) = 0.$$

Now observe that

$$E(U_{it}|d_i = 1) = \delta E(U_{ik}|d_i = 1) + E(\omega_{it}|d_i = 1).$$

But, as a consequence of assumption (c) above,

$$E(\omega_{it}|d_i = 1) = 0$$

since $E(\omega_{it}) = 0$ and because (c) guarantees that the mean of ω_{it} does not depend on X_{ik} and S_i. Similarly,

$$E(\omega_{it'}|d_i = 1) = 0$$

and thus condition (22) holds.

Linearity of the regression does not imply that the U_{it} are normally distributed (although if the U_{it} are joint normal, the regression is linear). The multivariate t density is just one example of many examples of densities with linear regressions.[20]

C. Anomalous Features of First Difference Estimators

Nearly all of the estimators require a control group (i.e., a sample of nontrainees). The only exception is the fixed effect estimator in a time homogeneous environment. In this case, if conditions (12) or (22) hold, if we let $X_{it}\beta = \beta_t$ to simplify the exposition, and if the environment is time homogeneous so $\beta_t = \beta_{t'}$, then

$$\hat{\alpha} = \overline{Y}_t^{(1)} - \overline{Y}_{t'}^{(0)}$$

consistently estimates α. The frequently stated claim that "if the environment is stationary, you don't need a control group" (see, e.g., Bassi, 1983) is false except for the special conditions which justify use of the fixed effect estimator.

Most of the procedures considered here can be implemented using only postprogram data. The covariance stationarity estimators of Sections VIC and VIIC, certain repeated cross-section estimators, and first difference methods constitute an exception to this rule. In this sense, those estimators are anomalous.

Fixed effect estimators are also robust to departures from the random sampling assumption. For instance, suppose conditions (12) or (22) are satisfied, but that the available data oversample or undersample trainees [i.e., the proportion of trainees in the sample does not converge to $p = E(d_i)$]. Suppose further that the analyst does not know the true value of p. Nevertheless, a first difference regression continues to identify α. Most other procedures do not share this property.

IX. Nonrandom Sampling Plans

Virtually all methods can be readily adjusted to account for choice-based sampling or measurement error in training status. Some methods require no modification at all.

The data available for analyzing the impact of training on earnings are often nonrandom samples. Frequently they consist of pooled data from two

---

[20] For reasons already discussed in footnote 14, the estimator proposed in this section is less attractive (and requires redefinition) in the context of estimating α^* in a random coefficient model.

sources: (a) a sample of trainees selected from program records and (b) a sample of nontrainees selected from some national sample. Typically, such samples overrepresent trainees relative to their proportion in the population. This creates the problem of choice-based sampling analyzed by Manski and Lerman (1977) and Manski and McFadden (1981).

A second problem, contamination bias, arises when the training status of certain individuals is recorded with error. Many control samples such as the Current Population Survey or Social Security Work History do not reveal whether or not persons have received training.

Both of these sampling situations combine the following types of data:

(A) earnings, earnings characteristics, and enrollment characteristics for a sample of trainees ($d_i = 1$);
(B) earnings, earnings characteristics, and enrollment characteristics for a sample of nontrainees ($d_i = 0$); and
(C) earnings, earnings characteristics, and enrollment characteristics for a national "control" sample of the population (e.g., CPS or Social Security records) where the training status of persons is not known.

If type (A) and (B) data are combined and the sample proportion of trainees does not converge to the population proportion of trainees, the combined sample is a choice-based sample. If type (A) and (C) data are combined with or without type (B) data, there is contamination bias because the training status of some persons is not known.

Most procedures developed in the context of random sampling can be modified to consistently estimate α using choice-based samples or contaminated control groups (i.e., groups in which training status is not known for individuals). In some cases, a consistent estimator of the population proportion of trainees is required. We illustrate these claims by showing how to modify the instrumental variables estimator to address both sampling schemes. Our companion paper gives explicit case by case treatment of these issues for each estimator developed there.

A. The Instrumental Variable (IV) Estimator: Choice-Based Sampling

If condition (9a) is strengthened to read

$$E(X'_{it}U_{it}|d_i) = 0$$
$$E(g(Z^e_i)U_{it}|d_i) = 0 \tag{24}$$

and a modified condition (9b) is also met, the IV estimator is consistent for α in choice-based samples.

To see why this is so, write the normal equations for the IV estimator in the following form:

$$
\begin{bmatrix}
\dfrac{\Sigma X_{it}'X_{it}}{I_t} & \dfrac{\Sigma X_{it}'d_i}{I_t} \\[2ex]
\dfrac{\Sigma g(Z_i^e)X_{it}}{I_t} & \dfrac{\Sigma g(Z_i^e)d_i}{I_t}
\end{bmatrix}
\begin{bmatrix} \hat{\beta} \\ \hat{\alpha} \end{bmatrix}
$$

$$
=
\begin{bmatrix}
\dfrac{\Sigma X_{it}'Y_{it}}{I_t} \\[2ex]
\dfrac{\Sigma g(Z_i^e)Y_{it}}{I_t}
\end{bmatrix}
\tag{25}
$$

$$
=
\begin{bmatrix}
\dfrac{\Sigma X_{it}'X_{it}}{I_t} & \dfrac{\Sigma X_{it}'d_i}{I_t} \\[2ex]
\dfrac{\Sigma g(Z_i^e)X_{it}}{I_t} & \dfrac{\Sigma g(Z_i^e)d_i}{I_t}
\end{bmatrix}
\begin{bmatrix} \beta \\ \alpha \end{bmatrix}
+
\begin{bmatrix}
\dfrac{\Sigma X_{it}'U_{it}}{I_t} \\[2ex]
\dfrac{\Sigma g(Z_i^e)U_{it}}{I_t}
\end{bmatrix}.
$$

Since condition (24) guarantees that

$$
\operatorname*{plim}_{I_t \to \infty} \frac{\Sigma X_{it}'U_{it}}{I_t} = 0 \quad \text{and}
$$

$$
\operatorname*{plim}_{I_t \to \infty} \frac{\Sigma g(Z_i^e)U_{it}}{I_t} = 0
\tag{26}
$$

and modified rank condition (9b) holds, the IV estimator is consistent.

In a choice-based sample, let the probability that an individual has enrolled in training be p^*. Even if conditions (9a) and (9b) are satisfied, there is no guarantee that condition (26) will be met without invoking condition (24). This is so because

$$
\operatorname*{plim}_{I_t \to \infty} \frac{\Sigma X_{it}'U_{it}}{I_t} = E(X_{it}'U_{it}|d_i = 1)p^* + E(X_{it}'U_{it}|d_i = 0)(1 - p^*)
$$

$$
\operatorname*{plim}_{I_t \to \infty} \frac{\Sigma g(Z_i^e)U_{it}}{I_t} = E(g(Z_i^e)U_{it}|d_i = 1)p^* + E(g(Z_i^e)U_{it}|d_i = 0)(1 - p^*).
$$

These expressions are not generally zero, so the IV estimator is generally inconsistent.

In the case of random sampling, $p^* = \Pr[d_i = 1] = p$ and the above expressions are identically zero. They are also zero if condition (24) is satisfied. However, it is not necessary to invoke condition (24). Provided p is known, it is possible to reweight the data to secure consistent estimators under the assumptions of Section IV. Multiplying equation (1) by the weight

$$\omega_i = d_i \frac{p}{p^*} + (1 - d_i)\left(\frac{1-p}{1-p^*}\right)$$

and applying IV to the transformed equation produces an estimator that satisfies condition (24). It is straightforward to check that weighting the sample at hand back to random sample proportions causes the IV method to consistently estimate α and β (see Heckman and Robb, 1985).

B. The IV Estimator: Contamination Bias

For data of type (C) (see beginning of Section IX), d_i is not observed. Applying the IV estimator to pooled samples (A) and (C) assuming that observations in (C) have $d_i = 0$ produces an inconsistent estimator. However, it is possible to construct a consistent estimator for this case.

In terms of the IV equations (25), from sample (C) it is possible to generate the cross products

$$\frac{\Sigma X'_{it} X_{it}}{I_c}, \qquad \frac{\Sigma g(Z_i^e) X_{it}}{I_c}, \qquad \frac{\Sigma X'_{it} Y_{it}}{I_c}, \qquad \frac{\Sigma g(Z_i^e) Y_{it}}{I_c},$$

which converge to the desired population counterparts where I_c denotes the number of observations in sample (C). Missing is information on the cross products

$$\frac{\Sigma X'_{it} d_i}{I_c}, \qquad \frac{\Sigma g(Z_i^e) d_i}{I_c}.$$

Notice that if d_i were measured accurately in sample (C),

$$\plim_{I_c \to \infty} \frac{\Sigma X'_{it} d_i}{I_c} = pE[X'_{it}|d_i = 1]$$

$$\plim_{I_c \to \infty} \frac{\Sigma g(Z_i^e) d_i}{I_c} = pE[g(Z_i^e)|d_i = 1].$$

But the means of X_{it} and $g(Z_i^e)$ in sample (A) converge to

$$E(X'_{it}|d_i = 1) \quad \text{and} \quad E(g(Z_i^e)|d_i = 1),$$

respectively. Hence, inserting the sample (A) means of X_{it} and $g(Z_i^e)$ multiplied by p in the second column of the matrix IV equations (25) produce a consistent IV estimator provided that in the limit the size of samples (A) and (C) both approach infinity.

C. Repeated Cross-Section Methods with Unknown Training Status and Choice-Based Sampling

The repeated cross-section estimators discussed in Section V are inconsistent when applied to choice-based samples unless additional conditions are assumed. For example, when the environment is time homogeneous and condition (12) also holds, $(\overline{Y}_t - \overline{Y}_{t'})/p$ remains a consistent estimator of α in choice-based samples as long as the same proportion of trainees are sampled in periods t' and t. If a condition such as condition (12) is not met, it is necessary to know the identity of trainees to weight the sample back to the proportion of trainees that would be produced by a random sample to obtain consistent estimators. Hence, the class of estimators that does not require knowledge of individual training status is not robust to choice-based sampling.

D. Control Function Estimators

A subset of cross-sectional and longitudinal procedures is robust to choice-based sampling. Those procedures construct a control function K_{it} with the following properties:

K_{it} depends on variables..., $Y_{i,t+1}$, Y_{it}, $Y_{i,t-1}, \ldots, X_{i,t+1}$, X_{it}, $X_{i,t-1},\ldots$, d_i and parameters ψ and
(a) $E(U_{it} - K_{it}|d_i, X_{it}, K_{it}, \psi) = 0$ (27)
(b) ψ is identified.

When inserted into the earnings function of equation (1), K_{it} purges the equation of dependence between U_{it} and d_i. Rewriting equation (1) to incorporate K_{it},

$$Y_{it} = X_{it}\beta + d_i\alpha + K_{it} + (U_{it} - K_{it}). \qquad (28)$$

The purged disturbance $(U_{it} - K_{it})$ is orthogonal to the right-hand side variables in the new equation. This (possibly nonlinear) regression applied to equation (28) consistently estimates the parameters (α, β, ψ). Moreover, condition (27) implies that $(U_{it} - K_{it})$ is orthogonal to the right-hand side variables conditional on d_i, X_{it} and K_{it}:

$$E(Y_{it}|X_{it}, d_i, K_{it}) = X_{it}\beta + d_i\alpha + K_{it}.$$

Thus, if type (A) and (B) data are combined in any proportion, least squares estimators of equation (28) consistently estimate (α, β, ψ) provided the number of trainees and nontrainees in the sample both approach infinity. The class of control function estimators which satisfies condition (27) can be implemented without modification in choice-based samples.

The sample selection bias methods (d)–(e) described in Section IVB and the propensity score methods formulated in Section X exploit the control function principle. Our companion paper gives further examples of control function estimators.

E. Summary and Conclusions on Robustness Properties

Repeated cross-section estimators which do not exploit knowledge of the training identity of persons are not robust to choice-based sampling nor can they be weighted to produce consistent estimators of α. (Repeated cross-section estimators with training identity known can obviously be reweighted to produce consistent estimators.) However, these estimators are robust to contamination bias provided that the population proportion of trainees is known or can be consistently estimated.

A major conclusion of our analysis is that with the exception of repeated cross-section estimators with the training status of persons unknown, using robustness to contamination bias or choice-based sampling as a criterion for selecting estimators does not suggest a clear ordering of cross-section, repeated cross-section, or longitudinal estimators. Control function estimators are robust to choice-based sampling, but such estimators can be formed on all three types of data sets.

X. The Propensity Score and Mixture Models as Solutions to the General Problem of Selection Bias

Under special conditions, the control function of condition (27) can be expressed as a function of the propensity score $\Pr(d_i = 1 | Z_i)$ and no other variables. If selection occurs only on observables, the control function of condition (27) can be expressed solely as a function of the propensity score. Propensity score methods offer no solution to the general problem of selection bias. The mixture modeling approach of Glynn et al. (1986) assumes access to data not usually available in analyzing problems of selection bias.

A. Propensity Score Methods

In a series of papers, Rosenbaum and Rubin (1983, 1985) have advocated the use of the propensity score $[\Pr(d_i = 1 | Z_i)]$ in a matching estimation method for controlling or reducing bias in observational studies. Some authors (e.g., Scheuren, 1985; Coleman, 1985) have proposed use of the propensity score as an alternative to more conventional selection bias methods. The propensity score methodology suggests use of $\Pr(d_i = 1 | Z_i)$ as a control function in a matching procedure.

Two distinct topics should be distinguished in evaluating this proposed "cure" for selection bias: (a) a statement of conditions under which there exists a control function that depends solely on the propensity score (and some parameters) and (b) the validity of matching methods. We do not discuss (b) in this paper.[21]

Assuming the existence of selection bias $[E(U_{it}d_i) \neq 0]$ and that X_{it} is distributed independently of U_{it} given Z_i, the propensity score methodology assumes in the fixed coefficient model that d_i and U_{it} are conditionally independent given Z_i and X_{it}

$$d_i \perp\!\!\!\perp U_{it} | (Z_i, X_{it}). \tag{29}$$

In a random coefficient model it assumes that

$$d_i \perp\!\!\!\perp (U_{it} + \epsilon_i d_i) | (Z_i, X_{it}).$$

We confine our discussion to the fixed coefficient case. The modifications required in our analysis for the random coefficient case are obvious.

For there to be a nontrivial selection problem $[E(U_{it}d_i) \neq 0]$ and for equation (29) to be satisfied, the only source of selection bias must be selection on the observables (as defined in Section IVE). Selection on unobservables is ruled out. Using the law of iterated expectations in the manner of Rosenbaum and Rubin (1983, Theorem 3), if equation (29) is true, then

$$\begin{aligned}
E\left[Y_{it} | d_i, X_{it}, \Pr(d_i = 1 | Z_i, X_{it})\right] \\
= X_{it}\beta + d_i\alpha + E\left[U_{it} | \Pr(d_i = 1 | Z_i, X_{it})\right].
\end{aligned} \tag{30}$$

The term $E[U_{it} | \Pr(d_i = 1 | Z_i, X_{it})]$ may be used as a control function in the sense of the definition of condition (27). Instead of conditioning on Z_i, X_{it}, it is sufficient to condition on $\Pr(d_i = 1 | Z_i, X_{it})$ in constructing a control function. If X_{it} is distributed independently of V_i given Z_i, then $\Pr(d_i = 1 | Z_i, X_{it}) = \Pr(d_i = 1 | Z_i)$ and the analysis may be conducted in terms of the propensity score defined in Section IIB. Thus, it is possible to reduce the scale of the matching problem if matching methods are used (assuming

---

[21] We note that the published literature on matching offers no formal proofs of any desirable property of matching estimators in the case in which regressor variables are continuously distributed (it is trivial to establish optimality properties for matching in the case in which all regressors are categorical with finite categories). Recent claims about the robustness of matching methods in the case in which the functional form of a regression model is unknown are not yet supported by published systematic theoretical arguments or by compelling Monte Carlo or empirical evidence. Assertions about the generality of matching methods remain to be substantiated. (See Barros, 1986, for some general theorems on the consistency and asymptotic normality of matching methods with continuous regressors.)

that X_{it} and Z_i are categorical variables with a finite number of categories) and consistent estimators of α are produced by matching. Otherwise, postulating the functional form of $E(U_{it}|\Pr(d_i = 1|Z_i, X_{it})]$, it is possible to use regression to consistently estimate α under conditions postulated in our companion paper.

A key assumption underlying the method is the existence of at least one regressor in the decision rule of equation (2). As noted in Section III, this rules out a completely nonparametric estimation strategy. However, Z_i need not be distributed independently of V_i, although in practice (e.g., Rosenbaum and Rubin, 1985) this is assumed to be the case with V_i logistically distributed. The repeated cross-section and longitudinal estimators, as well as the cross-section estimators that assume knowledge of the functional form of the distribution of U_{it} [or at least that $E(U_{it}^3) = E(U_{it}^5) = 0$] do not require any regressor in the decision rule.

Since Z_i is not independent of U_{it}, elements of Z_i are not, in general, valid instrumental variables for d_i, [see method (a) in Section IVB]. However, elements of Z_i may be uncorrelated with U_{it} and may be valid instruments. For the same reason, methods (b) and (c) of Section IVB are generally inappropriate. However, method (d) is still appropriate because as a consequence of equation (29),

$$E(U_{it}|d_i = 1, Z_i, X_{it}) = E(U_{it}|d_i = 0, Z_i, X_{it}) = E(U_{it}|Z_i, X_{it}).$$

By virtue of equation (30), one can condition on $\Pr(d_i = 1|Z_i, X_{it})$ rather than on Z_i, X_{it} to arrive at the special control function implicit in Rosenbaum and Rubin (1983).

Selection solely on the observables is a very special case of the general problem of selection bias. In the context of evaluating training programs, Z_i may be correlated with U_{it}, but U_{it} and V_i must be independent given Z_i. There can be no unobserved motivational or ability variables common to the equation governing the decision to enroll a person into training and the equation determining his or her potential earnings. In the context of Coleman's work on the choice between public and private schools, the propensity score methodology is valid if selection occurs solely on the observables so that there is no correlation between unobserved person-specific and family-specific motivational and ability factors that affect test outcomes and the decision to place a child in a private school. The propensity score methodology solves a very special problem (already considered by Barnow, et al., 1980) that is of limited interest to social science data analysts.

The propensity score can also be used (in a different way than that advocated by Rosenbaum and Rubin, 1983) in a setting in which there is selection on the unobservables but there is no selection on the observables (Z_i is independent of U_{it}) and Z_i and X_{it} are distributed independently of V_i, an assumption not required when there is selection solely on the observables. In this case, discussed in Heckman (1980) and our companion paper (p. 188),

$$E(U_{it}|d_i = 1, Z_i) = \frac{\int_{-\infty}^{\infty} u \int_{-Z_i\gamma}^{\infty} f(u, v)\, dv\, du}{\int_{-Z_i\gamma}^{\infty} f(v)\, dv}$$

$$E(U_{it}|d_i = 0, Z_i) = \frac{\int_{-\infty}^{\infty} u \int_{-\infty}^{-Z_i\gamma} f(v)\, dv}{\int_{-\infty}^{-Z_i\gamma} f(v)\, dv}$$

Using the facts that

$$\Pr(d_i = 0|Z_i) = 1 - F(-Z_i\gamma)$$
$$\Pr(d_i = 0|Z_i) = F(-Z_i\gamma)$$

and the strict monotonicity of F (a new assumption), we may write

$$E(U_{it}|d_i = 1, Z_i) = \frac{\int_{-\infty}^{\infty} u \int_{F^{-1}[1-\Pr(d_i=1|Z_i)]}^{\infty} f(u, v)\, dv\, du}{\Pr(d_i = 1|Z_i)}$$

$$= K_1[\Pr(d_i = 1|Z_i)]$$

$$E(U_{it}|d_i = 0, Z_i) = \frac{\int_{-\infty}^{\infty} u \int_{-\infty}^{F^{-1}[1-\Pr(d_i=1|Z_i)]} f(u, v)\, dv\, du}{\Pr(d_i = 0|Z_i)}$$

$$= K_0[\Pr(d_i = 0|Z_i)]$$

where

$$K_1\Pr(d_i = 1|Z_i) + K_0\Pr(d_i = 0|Z_i) = 0,$$

and where

$$K = K_1 d_i + K_0(1 - d_i)$$

is a control function in the sense of condition (27) and is a function solely of the propensity score.[22] Use of the propensity score in this fashion involves no new idea and is just an instance of estimator (d) given in Section IVB.

Note, however, that very different assumptions are required to justify this control function than are required to justify the control function for selection on observables implicit in Rosenbaum and Rubin (1983). Under the assumption that Z_i is distributed independently of U_{it} (or at least that one element of Z_i is uncorrelated with U_{it}), the appropriate elements of Z_i may be used as instruments for d_i, whereas they are invalid instruments under the assumptions of Rosenbaum and Rubin (1983) which produce a

---

[22] Under the null hypothesis of no selection bias, polynomials in $\Pr(d_i = 1|Z_i)$ should not appear in the regression of Y_{it} on X_{it} and d_i (Heckman, 1980). The same test with obvious modification in the conditioning set can be applied to the model of Rosenbaum and Rubin (1983) or Barnow et al. (1980). These are exact tests under the null hypothesis.

nontrivial selection bias problem.[23] Note further that is is possible to test between these two specifications provided a control function

$$E(U_{it}|X_{it}, Z_i, d_i=j) \qquad j=1,0$$

exists (see Heckman and Robb, 1985, p. 191). This control function can be used to produce consistent estimators of α for either model, whereas each of the other two control function estimators are invalid under the conditions assumed to justify the other.

B. Mixture Modeling

The "mixture modeling" approach advocated by Glynn et al. (this volume) at this conference assumes access to data not typically available in the analysis of selection bias models. Nonrespondents are randomly sampled in a follow-up sample and give information that suffices to determine the parameters of the outcome distribution for nonrespondents without bias. In our context, they assume that trainees can be randomly placed in non-trainee status for one period. By appropriately weighting estimates for respondents and nonrespondents it is possible to estimate population parameters without bias. A simple consistent weighted mean estimator exists for their model, although the authors do not explicitly present it. [It is implicitly given by choosing a $N(0, \infty)$ prior.]

The Glynn et al. (this volume) paper is disappointing to us because of the caricature it presents of econometric methods for solving selection bias problems. It reiterates a false statement frequently made in the statistics community that econometric selection bias procedures depend on normality assumptions or other strong distributional assumptions. It should be apparent to the reader of this paper and our companion paper that this caricature of econometric work is false.

The Glynn et al. paper considers a model in which respondents and nonrespondents are assumed to come from different distributions. In many choice-theoretic behavioral models it is much more natural to postulate that respondents and nonrespondents (or trainees and nontrainees) have outcomes drawn from a common distribution and that they use a common decision rule in making decisions albeit with different consequences. *Ex post*, not *ex ante*, distributions are different. Missing in their analysis is any explicit causal or behavioral mechanism generating the data.

Equations like our (1) and (2) can be used to characterize the population as a whole, define the parameters of behavioral interest, and provide the context within which it is possible to judge the plausibility of various

---

[23] If some elements of Z_i are not correlated with U_{it}, they may be valid instruments in the Rosenbaum and Rubin model provided that a rank condition is satisfied.

identifying restrictions. This formulation of the selection problem enables the analyst to clarify the explicit rules generating the selected samples.

XI. Summary

This paper presents alternative methods for estimating the impact of treatments on outcomes when nonrandom selection characterizes the enrollment of persons into treatment categories. In the absence of genuine experimental data, some assumptions must be invoked to solve the problem of selection bias. The choice of an appropriate assumption requires appeal to context, *a priori* beliefs, and prior knowledge. There is no context-free solution to the problem of selection bias despite apparent claims to the contrary in the recent literature in statistics which solves selection problems by imposing ad hoc mathematical structures onto the data.

We have defined the parameters of behavioral interest for a prototypical problem of estimating the impact of training on earnings. We have explored the benefits of having access to cross-section, repeated cross-section, and longitudinal data by considering the assumptions required to use a variety of new and conventional estimators to identify the behavioral parameters of interest. We state just-identifying assumptions which cannot be tested with data and compare those with overidentifying assumptions which in principle are testable. We examine the plausibility of these assumptions when viewed in the light of prototypical decision rules determining the enrollment of persons into training. Since specification of decision rules is an inherently controversial issue, we consider the robustness of various estimators to ignorance about the decision process. Because many samples are choice-based samples and because the problem of measurement error is pervasive, we examine the robustness of estimators to choice based sampling and measurement error.

We find that cross-section selection bias estimators do not require the elaborate distributional assumptions frequently invoked in practice. Such conventional overidentifying assumptions are in principle testable.

A key conclusion of our analysis is that the benefits of longitudinal data have been overstated in the recent literature because a false comparison has been made. Repeated cross-section data can often be used to identify the same parameters as can be identified in longitudinal data. Uniquely longitudinal estimators require assumptions that are different from the assumptions required to justify cross-section or repeated cross-section estimators.

We also consider propensity score methods and mixture modeling approaches recently advocated as solutions to the selection problem in the statistics literature. We find that the propensity score method solves the problem of selection bias for the case in which selection occurs solely on observable characteristics. Mixture modeling, as presented at this conference, assumes access to data typically not available. When it does not (as in Rubin, 1977), it solves the problem of selection bias by invoking normality assumptions.

Any just-identified solution to the problem of selection bias in nonexperimental data requires an appeal to principles or assumptions that cannot be tested with data. Behavioral social scientists often appeal to context, beliefs, and *a priori* theory. Statisticians tend to substitute ad hoc mathematical assumptions in place of contextual assumptions. Such mathematical assumptions contain implicit behavioral premises, but these are rarely stated. Until these implicit behavioral assumptions are made explicit and the limitations of mathematical statistics are clearly recognized, there will be no convergence in views on the validity, and limits, of competing approaches to the selection bias problem. The "solution" to the selection bias problem lies outside of formal statistics.

Acknowledgments. . This research was supported by NSF SES-8107963 and NIH-1-R01-HD16846-01 to the Quantitative Economics Group at NORC. Heckman is affiliated with that group and the Department of Economics at the University of Chicago. Robb is affiliated with NORC and the Chicago Corporation. We have benefited from helpful comments made by Stephen Stigler and members of the Statistics Workshop at the University of Chicago. We also thank John Tukey for his comments at the ETS Conference and for very helpful correspondence. Don Rubin is also thanked for his comments. Ricardo Barros made especially helpful comments on several drafts of this paper.

Bibliography

Amemiya, T. (1981). "Qualitative response models: A survey." *J. Econ. Lit.*, 19, 1483–1536.

Ashenfelter, O. (1978). "Estimating the effect of training programs on earnings." *Rev. Econ. Statist.*, 60, 47–57.

Barnow, B., Cain, G., and Goldberger, A. (1980). "Issues in the analysis of selectivity bias." In E. Stromsdorfer and G. Farkas (eds.), *Evaluation Studies*, vol. 5. San Francisco: Sage.

Barros, R. (1986). *Three Essays on Selection and Identification Problems in Economics*. Ph.D. thesis, University of Chicago, Chicago, Illinois.

Bassi, L. (1983). *Estimating the Effect of Training Programs with Nonrandom Selection*. Ph.D. thesis, Princeton University, Princeton, New Jersey.

Chamberlain, G. (1982). "Multivariate regression models for panel data." *J. Econometrics*, 18, 1–46.

Coleman, J.C. (1985). "Schools, families and children." Ryerson Lecture, University of Chicago, April 1985.

Cox, D.R. *The Planning of Experiments*. New York: John Wiley, (1958).

Dawid, A.P. (1979). "Conditional independence in statistical theory" (with discussion). *J. Roy. Statist. Soc. Ser. B*, 41, 1–31.

Fienberg, S., Singer, B., and Tanur, J. (1985). "Large-scale social experimentation in the United States." In A.C. Atkinson and S. Fienberg (eds.), *A Celebration of Statistics*. Berlin/New York: Springer-Verlag.

Fisher, R.A. (1953). *The Design of Experiments*. London: Hafner.

Goldfeld, S. and Quandt, R. (1976). "Techniques for estimating switching regressions." In S. Goldfeld and R. Quandt (eds.), *Studies in Nonlinear Estimation*. Cambridge, Massachusetts: Ballinger.

Heckman, J. (1976). "Simultaneous equations models with continuous and discrete endogenous variables and structural shifts." In S. Goldfeld and R. Quandt (eds.), *Studies in Nonlinear Estimation*. Cambridge, Massachusetts: Ballinger.

Heckman, J. "Dummy endogenous variables in a simultaneous equations system." *Econometrica*, 46, 931–961.

Heckman, J. (1979). "Sample selection bias as a specification error." *Econometrica*, 47, 153–161.

Heckman, J. (1980). "Addendum to sample selection bias as a specification error." In E. Stromsdorfer and G. Farkas (eds.), *Evaluation Studies*, vol. 5. San Francisco: Sage.

Heckman, J. and Neumann, G. (1977). "Union wage differentials and the decision to join unions." Unpublished manuscript, University of Chicago, Chicago, Illinois.

Heckman, J. and Robb, R. (1985). "Alternative methods for evaluating the impact of interventions." In J. Heckman and B. Singer (eds.), *Longitudinal Analysis of Labor Market Data.*, New York: Cambridge University Press, pp. 156–245.

Heckman, J. and Wolpin, K. (1976). "Does the contract compliance program work?: An analysis of Chicago data." *Indust. Labor Relations Rev.*, 19, 415–433.

Lee, L.F. (1978). "Unionism and wage rates: A simultaneous equations model with qualitative and limited dependent variables." *Intl. Econ. Rev.*, 19, 415–433.

Little, R.J. (1985). "A note about models for selectivity bias." *Econometrica*, 53(6), 1469–1474.

MaCurdy, T. (1982). "The use of time series processes to model the error structure of earnings in a longitudinal data analysis." *J. Econometrics*, 18(1), 83–114.

Manski, C. and Lerman, S. (1977). "The estimation of choice probabilities from choice-based samples." *Econometrica*, 45, 1977–1988.

Manski, C. and McFadden, D. (1981). "Alternative estimators and sample designs for discrete choice analysis." In C. Manski and D. McFadden (eds.), *Structural Analysis of Discrete Data with Econometric Applications*. Cambridge, Massachusetts: MIT Press, pp. 117–136.

Mundlak, Y. (1961). "Empirical production functions free of management bias." *J. Farm Econometrics*, 43, 45–56.

Mundlak, Y. (1978). "On the pooling of time series and cross section data." *Econometrica*, 46, 69–85.

Rosenbaum, P. and Rubin, D. (1983). "The central role of the propensity score in observational studies for causal effects." *Biometrika*, 70, 41–55.

Rosenbaum, P. and Rubin, D. (1985). "Constructing a control group using multivariate sampling methods that incorporate the propensity score." *Amer. Statist.*, 39(1), 33–38.

Roy, A. (1951). "Some thoughts on the distribution of earnings." *Oxford Econ. Pap.*, 3, 135–146.

Rubin, D. (1977). "Formalizing subjective notions about the effects of nonrespondents in sample surveys." *J. Amer. Statist. Assoc.*, 72(359), 538–543.

Scheuren, F. (1985). "Evaluating manpower training: Some notes on data handling issues." Report to JTLS Panel, U.S. Department of Labor, Washington, D.C.

Simon, H. (1957). "Spurious correlation: A causal interpretation." In H. Simon (ed.), *Models of Man*. New York: John Wiley, 37–49.

Comments by John W. Tukey

(1) The revised paper shows an extremely commendable attempt to make things readable. Real progress has been made. (I know some statistician's survey papers on regression that are considerably harder to read than the new version.) As a result, I have at least read the words in the new version, and I feel I have an appreciably clearer idea of what is going on. (In particular, I *have* read the introduction, presumably the important eighth of the paper, to which my comments are directed.) This has not left me more comfortable, as I now explain.

(2) Some of my deepest discomfort stems from the feeling that the authors equate "assumption" to "truth." If we assume it, it is so—if we don't, it isn't! It could be argued that this feeling is not fully justified, but then the authors say, a third of the way through the introduction, "If that assumption is not made, then the problem of selection bias disappears." They can only have equated "is not made" with "is not true." Is this making "truth" also a matter of "context, belief, and *a priori* theory"?

(3) A similar point appears just after their Equation (8), where they say, "one way to acquire information...is (to) assume...," which clearly equates assumption to information (and presumably to fact).

(4) So far as I can tell, the authors' words "any behavioral theory" mean "any simple normative principle, expressed as a detailed decision rule based on anticipated gain." I think better of behavioral science than to make this identification. As one extreme example, could any such "anticipated gain" theory account for theological schools?

(5) The view seems to be taken that any assumption not needed for "identification" is "unnecessarily strong." We really want useful answers, not bare identifications. We do not yet know which of these assumptions are important, nay even essential, for getting useful answers. Yet the authors say "separating out essential from inessential assumptions is a main goal of this paper" in which they appear to mean "essential for identification," but they in fact mean "essential for consistent estimation." They do spend a paragraph almost, but not quite, saying that, in this paper, "identification" means "demonstrating the possibility of consistent estimation by simple statistics." As a consequence, perhaps, "consistent estimation" appears in a few other sentences in the introduction. But we are never reminded, for instance, that "minimal identifying assumptions" really means "minimal assumptions to make certain combinations of means (or other simple statistics) consistent estimators." Clarifying this issue throughout the introduction could lead to clumsy wording, though it could greatly help the reader. Perhaps some shorthand like "c-identification," "c-identify," and the like would have made it possible to regularly remind the reader what is really going on without great awkwardness.

(6) One has to be uncomfortable about the authors' use of, and attitude toward, *testability*. On the one hand, anything not needed for identification

—really not needed for consistent estimation—is labeled "testable" and then automatically shunned. It is bothersome to see "testable" as a reason for rejection. On the other, the desirable term *testable* seems to mean only "there has to be some parameter that can be consistently estimated in some way that vanishes when the additional assumption holds." Even with such a parameter, and such an estimate in our hands, we would still need something like a well-developed sampling theory to tell us how to interpret estimate values for given amounts of underlying data. One may hope that such a sampling theory might eventually come to pass, but when? A phrase like "eventually testable" might convey a more accurate picture.

(7) A little later, the authors take a couple of paragraphs on "efficiency." I would like to see a discussion about "variance" instead. The question is "How much data do we need before the method we have thought of will give results of useful accuracy?" not "How much better we might conceivably do, possibly by exploiting some idiosyncracy of an assumption we do not really trust?"

(8) At the close of these two paragraphs the authors say "For the topic of this paper—model identification—the efficiency issue is a red herring." Yet in the immediately following paragraph, they return to their love affair with cross-sectional data, arguing that only 10 times as much cross-sectional data as longitudinal data "may" swamp intrinsic differences in precision. Is this following a red herring? Is there any reason to suppose that a factor of 10 is enough? That 100 or 1000 times as much data might not be needed to swamp the longitudinal results? (I think every "may" in this paragraph and the next would better read "might"!)

(9) The authors stress the expense of collecting longitudinal data free of attrition bias, but give no consideration of whether we can, or how we might, keep this bias out of cross-sectional studies.

(10) I have very great discomfort with their attitude toward experimentation. The introduction's opening sentence, in view of footnote 8, presumably assumes that laboratory experiments give perfect data. They do not. They have weaknesses, just as social science experiments do. Apparently, the authors either fear—or are strongly repelled from—the idea of confirmation as the final standard of correctness (I should like to understand why). There are many social science areas where confirmation is either routinely demanded or at least taken as the ultimate standard. And what would Alfred Marshall have thought?

(11) "Causality" for the authors is clearly quite different from "causality" for the great bulk of physical scientists and engineers, for whom the essence is a combination of continued empirical relationship with the ruling out of other causal patterns. To say that causal interpretations are resolved by "context, beliefs, and *a priori* theory" is to demote causal interpretations to the level of transient opinions or fads. Much great progress in physical science has come from destroying unfounded beliefs (like spontaneous generation) and widely accepted *a priori* theory (like falling bodies before

Galileo). Presumably judgments of causality are the most important judgments economists are called on to make—shouldn't they be well founded?

(12) For all the seriousness of these negatives, the authors deserve our thanks for valiant efforts to clarify and expose important issues. Their introduction has done an excellent job of revealing both their thinking and the framework in which it operates. While it may be thought to make it too easy to criticize both thinking and framework, the introduction is a yeoman service for all those who need to understand thinking and framework as an essential background to the details that follow.

Postscript: A Rejoinder to Tukey

In his written comments on this paper, John Tukey strongly objects to our interpretation of the role of subjective, nonempirical conventions and beliefs in deciding among alternative causal interpretations of social science data. He writes "to say that causal interpretations are resolved by 'context, beliefs, and *a priori* theory' is to demote causal interpretations to the level of transient opinions or fads." He also states that "the authors fear—or are strongly repelled from—the idea of confirmation as the final standard of correctness." He further writes that "some of my deepest discomfort stems from the feeling that the authors equate 'assumption' to 'truth.' If we assume it, it is so—if we don't, it isn't!"

We greatly appreciate Professor Tukey's honest reaction to our work, but we are somewhat surprised by it. In writing our paper, we assumed that readers of our paper were familiar with a huge body of theoretical work on the "identification problem" which considers alternative *subjective* or non-verifiable assumptions *required* to move from statements about empirical correlations or associations to causal inference about empirical relationships. Since the time of Working (1927), Koopmans et al. (1950), Simon (1957), and Blalock (1961), social scientists have been aware of the point that empirical relationships estimated from nonexperimental data cannot be interpreted causally without invoking explicit assumptions. The problem of spurious correlation haunts such analyses. Causal relationships can be estimated *in principle* from *ideal* experimental data in which all other factors but the one being studied are held constant. Without such data, the observation that two outcomes are correlated is consistent with a variety of causal stories.

Identifying assumptions *are not empirically testable* provided that they "just" identify the model. Identifying assumptions *inevitably* are subjective until they are subject to experimental confirmation. To state this as a fact is not to be pleased with the state of affairs created by the fact. Tukey accuses us of "demoting" causal interpretations in social science. This is not so. We simply recognize the basis for such inference. We are asking people who make such interpretations to be clear about assumptions that give rise to their particular interpretation. As practicing social scientists, we feel that the point we are making is *not* sufficiently well appreciated by many of our empirically oriented colleagues. The conditional nature of the evidence on causal models is often overlooked. Competing social science paradigms are often just alternative normalizations of the same data. The existing data are consistent with very different views. If social scientists were forced to make their identifying assumptions explicit, a lot of fruitless empirical work on "causal" models would be eliminated and the theological, philosophical, or political beliefs that motivate alternative views (and alternative identifying assumptions) and that ultimately are the source of much controversy in social science would more quickly come to light.

In our opinion, the empirical statuses of causal and descriptive models are fundamentally different. In science this distinction is less clear cut because of access to experiments that *in principle* (although clearly not always in practice) permit causal models to be tested with data.

There are genuine empirical regularities in social science and these can be established without appealing to identifying assumptions. However, most of the attention of social scientists is increasingly focused on causal interpretation. At its core, this activity is premised on untestable assumptions although the literature in social science rarely makes this point clear. Our paper is an attempt to clarify the role of these assumptions within a class of social science models designed to solve the problem of selection bias. The selection problem is *premised* on the existence of a causal model as discussed in Section II of our paper. Identification is prior to confirmation in causal models.

We do not focus on "testing" or "variance" or "efficiency" issues in our paper because these are secondary to the main concern of our paper. Before any causal inference can be drawn, *assumptions must be made*. This essential point is the main point of our paper. In causal models, data are often ultimately used to *illustrate* beliefs and not test them.

With all due respect to Professor Tukey, we feel that he is not sufficiently familiar with the quality of mainstream empirical work in social science. We suspect that he assumes that social scientists have access to the same quality of data and hold the same respect for data and disciplined empirical research as physical scientists.

When he writes "there are many social science areas where confirmation is either routinely demanded or at least taken as the ultimate standard" he ignores the prior preempirical nature of identifying assumptions in causal models. In our experience, many of the most empirically oriented "confirmationists" are blind to the conditional subjective nature of their empirical "truths." Our paper is designed to emphasize this point for an important class of causal social science models. Perhaps our goal is too limited. But any careful follower of the fruitless empirical controversies about "equilibrium versus disequilibrium," "Keynesian versus rational expectations models," or "human capital versus dual labor markets" will recognize that the real differences between proponents of these causal models cannot be settled with data. If participants in these empirical controversies were forced to make their assumptions and tests clear, they would realize that their differences cannot and will not be settled by the available (nonexperimental) data.[24] This is not to deny the valuable role of

---

[24] Of course, the same remarks apply to other areas of knowledge not based on experimental data (e.g., the controversy between "punctuated" versus gradual evolutionary development in evolutionary biology).

careful description in social science, but only to separate this activity from the intrinsically subjective activity of "building" or "testing" causal models in the social sciences.

We regret that Professor Tukey chooses to ignore the main point of our paper. Many of his comments on our paper are peripheral to its main point: exposing identifying assumptions and considering tradeoffs in such assumptions.

As empirical social scientists we are not pleased that *at its core* one aspect of empirical social science—causal modeling—is based on subjective assumptions which *cannot* be tested with the available data. Nonetheless, we feel that it is important to make this point clearly so that the true nature of such empirical knowledge is apparent. The fact that there is so little convergence in views among rival social scientists on so many topics on which so much empirical work has been done is empirical evidence in support of our concern. Like it or not, much social science research is "transient opinions or fads" because the issues involved *cannot* be resolved with existing data.

One final note. We are accused of equating "assumption" to "truth." This point convinces us that Tukey has chosen to ignore the main point of our paper. In our paper we equate "assumption" to "normalization." No single assumption is the "right" or "true" one. Each just-identifying assumption can explain the data equally well. Tukey seems to believe there is a universal "true" model for all selection problems. If that is so, we welcome an explicit statement of such a model from a statistician and scientist as eminent and insightful as John Tukey.

Bibliography

Blalock, H.M. (1961). *Causal Inferences in Nonexperimental Research*. Chapel Hill: University of North Carolina Press.

Koopmans, T.C., Rubin, H., and Leipnik, R.B. (1950). "Measuring the equation systems of dynamic economics." In T.C. Koopmans (ed.), *Statistical Inference in Dynamic Economic Models*, Cowles Commission Monograph 10. New York: John Wiley.

Simon, H.A. (1957). "Causal ordering and identifiability." In H. Simon (ed.), *Models of Man*. New York: John Wiley.

Working, E.J. (1927). "What do statistical 'demand curves' show?" *Quart. J. Econ.*, 41(1).

Selection Modeling Versus Mixture Modeling with Nonignorable Nonresponse

ROBERT J. GLYNN, NAN M. LAIRD, AND DONALD B. RUBIN

I. Introduction

It is sometimes suspected that nonresponse to a sample survey is related to the primary outcome variable. This is the case, for example, in studies of income or of alcohol consumption behaviors. If nonresponse to a survey is related to the level of the outcome variable, then the sample mean of this outcome variable based on the respondents will generally be a biased estimate of the population mean. If this outcome variable has a linear regression on certain predictor variables in the population, then ordinary least squares estimates of the regression coefficients based on the responding units will generally be biased unless nonresponse is a stochastic function of these predictor variables. The purpose of this paper is to discuss the performance of two alternative approaches, the selection model approach and the mixture model approach, for obtaining estimates of means and regression estimates when nonresponse depends on the outcome variable. Both approaches extend readily to the situation when values of the outcome variable are available for a subsample of the nonrespondents, called "follow-ups." The availability of follow-ups are a feature of the example we use to illustrate comparisons.

Selection models have been developed to address the problems of selectivity bias in observational studies as well as bias due to nonrandom nonresponse. Lee (1979), Olsen (1980), Heckman (1974, 1976, 1979), and Heckman and Robb (1985) have contributed to the development of selection models. We consider here the version of the selection model proposed by Greenlees et al. (1982) to obtain consistent linear regression estimates when response depends on the outcome. Their approach is to obtain maximum likelihood estimates from the joint likelihood of the linear regression parameters and the parameters of an assumed logistic response function. It is recognized that estimation in selection models is sensitive to the unobserved distribution of the outcome (Little, 1982). Okafor (1982) argued that all of the parameters in the joint likelihood proposed by Greenlees et al. (1982) cannot be reliably estimated. His approach was to specify the coefficient of the outcome in the logistic response function and then estimate other parameters. The amount of variability in the linear regression parameters as this coefficient ranges over a number of reasonable values provides some measure of the sensitivity of these regression parameters to nonignorable nonresponse. Evidence supporting the view presented by Okafor has been provided by Murnane et al. (1985) who described the high degree of sensitivity of related selection models to departures from underlying assumptions. Nonetheless, Greenlees et al. obtained reasonable parameter estimates in a situation where it was possible to evaluate the performance of estimation under their approach. The availability of a sample of follow-ups should also improve the performance of this approach.

Rubin (1977) proposed a different approach to the estimation of population means or regression parameters when nonresponse depends on the outcome variable. His approach extends the classic double sampling approach to a Bayesian framework (Cochran, 1977; Hansen and Hurwitz, 1946). Assume respondents and nonrespondents are separate populations with different regressions holding in each population. Parameters for nonrespondents can be estimated using prior assumptions about the relationship between the parameters of the respondents and the nonrespondents. If a sample of follow-ups is available, then these data can be used to estimate parameters for nonrespondents. Multiple imputation of values for nonrespondents who are not followed-up allows for more accurate estimation of the variability of regression estimates (Herzog and Rubin, 1983). Treating the total population as a mixture of respondents and nonrespondents allows for estimation of overall population parameters.

Our goal here is to examine the robustness of the selection model approach and compare it to the mixture model approach in the situation when there is a sample of follow-ups. Section II describes models and presents notation, and Section III describes data sets. Sections IV and V consider the selection model approach in simple situations when there are no regressors or only one regressor X. Two artificial data sets are used in this evaluation. In Section VI we evaluate the improvement in estimation under the selection model approach when Y values are obtained on a sample of nonrespondents. Section VII contains a description of mixture modeling estimation with follow-ups. Section VIII compares the application of both approaches to the estimation of the differences in alcohol consumption levels between retirees and workers among a population of men in the greater Boston area (Glynn et al., 1985).

II. Models and Notation

Let Y denote the outcome variable of interest and X a vector of predictor variables. Assume that in the population of interest Y_i has a regression on X_i:

$$Y_i = X_i\beta + \epsilon_i,$$

where ϵ_i is a normally distributed random disturbance with zero mean and constant variance σ^2 and is uncorrelated with ϵ_j for $i \neq j$. Assume levels of X are available for all sampled units but that not all sampled units respond to the survey and nonresponse is related to Y. We use both the selection model approach and the mixture model approach to obtain estimates of β in this situation.

The selection model approach assumes that the probability of response is a logistic function of Y and other variables Z:

$$P(R_i = 1 | Y_i, Z_i) = \exp(\alpha_0 + \alpha_1 Y_i + \gamma Z_i) / [1 + \exp(\alpha_0 + \alpha_1 Y_i + \gamma Z_i)],$$

where R_i is a response indicator equal to zero if individual i is a nonrespondent and equal to one if a respondent. The vector Z may include some or all of the components of X and may also include some other predictors. As with X, assume that values of Z are available for all sampled units. The joint likelihood of the linear regression parameters and the parameters of the logistic response function can be specified. If individual i is a respondent then the contribution to the likelihood is

$$L_i = \sigma^{-1}\Phi[(Y_i - X_i\beta)/\sigma]\exp(\alpha_0 + \alpha_1 Y_i + \gamma Z_i)/[1 + \exp(\alpha_0 + \alpha_1 Y_i + \gamma Z_i)].$$

Here Φ denotes the standard normal density function. If individual i is a nonrespondent, then the contribution to the likelihood is

$$L_i = \int \sigma^{-1}\Phi[(Y_i - X_i\beta)/\sigma] \Big/ [1 + \exp(\alpha_0 + \alpha_1 Y_i + \gamma Z_i)] \, dY.$$

This integral cannot be exactly evaluated so we approximated it by ten point Gauss–Hermite quadrature obtaining an approximate contribution to the likelihood for a nonrespondent of

$$L_i \simeq \sum_{j=1}^{10} A_j \Big/ \left\{\sqrt{\pi}\left[1 + \exp\left(\alpha_0 + \sqrt{2}\,\sigma\alpha_1 R_j + \alpha_1 X_i\beta + \gamma Z_i\right)\right]\right\},$$

where A_j are the coefficients and R_j are the roots of the tenth degree Hermite polynomial (Davis and Rabinowitz, 1984). If individual i is a nonrespondent whose Y value is later obtained by following up some of the nonrespondents then the contribution to the likelihood is

$$L_i = \sigma^{-1}\Phi[(Y_i - X_i\beta)/\sigma]/[1 + \exp(\alpha_0 + \alpha_1 Y + \gamma Z_i)].$$

To obtain maximum likelihood estimates, the log of the likelihood over all sampled units as a function of β, σ, α_0, α_1, and γ is maximized.

Three different algorithms were used to maximize this log likelihood. Both of the nonlinear regression programs in the BMDP statistical package (Dixon, 1981) were tried. One of these requires the analytic specification of the derivatives of the log likelihood, while the other numerically approximates derivatives which need not be specified. The third algorithm was a combination search and quasi-Newton algorithm for constrained minimization which is available in IMSL (International Mathematical and Statistical Library, 1982). This program does about four iterations of a derivative free maximization algorithm with each of 20 starting points. The 5 that result in the lowest values of the function are allowed to continue to convergence. In each estimation technique parameters were constrained to facilitate convergence.

Estimates of population means and regression coefficients when a sample of follow-ups are available were also obtained using mixture models. Methods used were extensions of methods described by Rubin (1977) and Herzog and Rubin (1983) when no follow-ups are available. We first describe mixture modeling estimates of sample means. Assume that respondents and nonrespondents are sampled from different normal distributions. In a simple random sample of n units on variable Y, suppose n_1 units are respondents, n_0 units are nonrespondents, and a sample of n_{01} of the nonrespondents are followed up. Assume noninformative prior distributions for the mean and variance of the respondents. For the application we consider, n_1 is large enough so that reasonably diffuse priors would be dominated by the data. The posterior mean and variance for respondents will be $\bar{y}_R$ and s_R^2/n_1, respectively, where $\bar{y}_R$ is the sample mean and s_R^2 is the sample variance for the n_1 respondents. Let μ_0 and σ_0^2 be the prior mean and variance for nonrespondents. The posterior mean for nonrespondents, taking follow-ups into consideration, will then be

$$\bar{y}_{NRP} = \left(\mu_0/\sigma_0^2 + n_{01}\bar{y}_{NR}/s_{NR}^2\right)\Big/\left(1/\sigma_0^2 + n_{01}/s_{NR}^2\right),$$

where $\bar{y}_{NR}$ and s_{NR}^2 are the sample mean and variance, respectively, for the nonrespondents who were followed up. It is assumed here that the variance among nonrespondents is fixed at s_{NR}^2. The posterior variance for nonrespondents is

$$\text{var}(\bar{y}_{NRP}) = \left(1/\sigma_0^2 + n_{01}/s_{NR}^2\right)^{-1}.$$

The mean of Y in the entire population is

$$p_1\mu_R + (1 - p_1)\mu_{NR},$$

where μ_R is the mean of the respondents, μ_{NR} is the mean of the nonrespondents, and p_1 is the proportion of respondents in the population.

An estimate for this mean is the weighted average of the posterior means

$$\bar{y} = (n_1/n)\bar{y}_R + (n_0/n)\bar{y}_{NRP}.$$

To estimate the variance of this mean, assume that $E(p_1|n_1) = n_1/n$ and var$(p_1|n_1) = n_1 n_0/n^3$. The estimated variance of this weighted mean is

$$(n_1/n)^2(s_R^2/n_1) + (n_0/n)^2 \text{var}(\bar{y}_{NRP}) + (\bar{y}_R - \bar{y}_{NRP})^2 n_0 n_1/n^3.$$

The last term in the sum is the contribution to the variance added because the proportion of respondents is estimated in the sample. Specifically, it is

$$\text{var}[E(\bar{y}|p_1)].$$

When the goal is estimation of linear regression parameters, we use multiple imputation (Rubin, 1978, 1985) to obtain mixture model estimates. This approach makes use of the knowledge of levels of predictors X for nonrespondents. Five imputations were made for each nonrespondent who was not followed up in order to estimate the variance between imputations. Imputed values were merged with known values to form five data sets with no missing values. In each of these five data sets, standard ordinary least squares regression was used to estimate the regression coefficients for the entire population. These five estimates were then averaged to obtain the multiple imputation estimates. Theory in Rubin (1986) shows that this approach simulates the answer that would have been obtained by the analytic extension of the mixture model approach with no covariates. Practical details are now described.

Assume nonrespondents have different regression parameters than respondents so that if unit i is a nonrespondent,

$$Y_i = X_i \beta_{NR} + \epsilon_i,$$

where ϵ_i is a normally distributed random disturbance with zero mean and constant variance σ_{NR}^2 and is uncorrelated with ϵ_j for $i \neq j$. Let m be the length of the vector β_{NR} and, as above, let n_{01} be the number of follow-ups. Using ordinary least squares, data from the n_{01} follow-ups were used to obtain estimated regression parameters b_{NR} and an estimated mean squared error s_{NR}^2 for the regression among nonrespondents. The true mean squared error σ_{NR}^2 is assumed to be distributed as

$$s_{NR}^2(n_{01} - m)/\chi^2(n_{01} - m \text{ degrees of freedom}),$$

and the regression parameters β_{NR} given σ_{NR}^2 are assumed to be distributed as

$$N\left(b_{NR}, \sigma_{NR}^2(X'X)^{-1}\right),$$

where X is the $m \times n_{01}$ design matrix. These are the posterior distributions of these parameters given noninformative prior distributions. Five draws were made from the χ^2 distribution with $n_{01} - m$ degrees of freedom in order to generate five values of σ_{NR}^2. Using these five drawn values of σ_{NR}^2, five draws of β_{NR} were made. For each of the $n_0 - n_{01}$ nonrespondents who were not followed up and each of these five drawn values of the nonrespondents' regression parameters, one value was drawn from the distribution of Y given that individual's known value of X. Imputed values for nonrespondents who were not followed up were merged with data from respondents and follow-ups to produce five complete data sets. In each of these five data sets, values for respondents and follow-ups were identical to their observed values. For each of the five data sets, ordinary least squares was used to obtain estimates of the linear regression of Y on X. Let $b_i = (b_{0i}, b_{1i}, \ldots, b_{m-1\,i})$, for $i = 1, \ldots, 5$, denote the ith regression estimate, and let $\mathrm{var}(b_i) = [\mathrm{var}(b_{0i}), \mathrm{var}(b_{1i}), \ldots, \mathrm{var}(b_{m-1\,i})]$ denote the estimated standard errors of this estimate. The mixture model estimate of the regression coefficients in the entire population is then

$$b = \left(\sum_{i=1}^{5} b_i \right) \Big/ 5.$$

The variance of these regression estimates is the sum of the average variance of estimation given one set of imputed values and the variance of the estimates across the multiple imputations. Specifically, let

$$U = \sum_{i=1}^{5} \mathrm{var}(b_i)/5,$$

and

$$W = \sum_{i=1}^{5} (b_i - b)(b_i - b)'/4.$$

Then the estimate of the variance of the regression parameters is

$$U + 6W/5.$$

The correction factor $6/5$ derives from a more careful argument for a small number of imputations (Rubin, 1986). The ratio of the variance across estimates to the sum of the average variance of estimation and the variance across estimates, $W/(U + W)$ where the vectors are divided elementwise, gives an estimate of the percentage of missing information for each of the components of β, which can be formalized to Fisher information (Rubin, 1986).

III. Data Sets

The initial evaluation of the performance of the selection model and the mixture model approaches contained in Sections IV–VII used artificial data generated from known distributions. All artificial data were generated using the random function generator in the SAS statistical package (SAS Institute, 1982). Draws from the χ^2 distribution required for multiple imputation also used this random function generator.

To illustrate the performance of the selection model and mixture model approaches when there are no covariates (see Sections IV, VI, and VII), we generated two artificial data sets as follows. Using the random function generator in the SAS statistical package, 400 random observations from a normal distribution with mean zero and variance one and 400 random observations from a distribution uniformly distributed on the interval $(0, 1)$ were generated. Denoting the normally distributed observations by Y_i and the uniformly distributed observations by U_i, an observation Y_i was classified as responding ($R_i = 1$) if

$$\exp(1 + Y_i)\big/\big[1 + \exp(1 + Y_i)\big] \geq U_i$$

and as nonresponding ($R_i = 0$) otherwise. This assumes that the response function is logistic with parameters $\alpha_0 = 1$ and $\alpha_1 = 1$. A second data set with a lognormal distribution was obtained by exponentiating all of the Y_i. This data set was assumed to have a logistic response function with parameters $\alpha_0 = 0$ and $\alpha_1 = 1$, chosen so that the overall response rate for the two data sets would be approximately equal. Units in this data set were considered responding if

$$\exp\big[\exp(Y_i)\big]\big/\big\{1 + \exp\big[\exp(Y_i)\big]\big\} \geq U_i$$

and as nonresponding otherwise.

Summary statistics for the generated data are shown in Table 1, and estimated parameters of the response functions are shown in Table 2. Because $\alpha_1 = 1$ in both data sets, units with large Y values are more likely to be respondents. The theoretical mean of the lognormally distributed data

Table 1. Sample moments of generated data[a]

		Normal data			Lognormal data	
	N	Sample mean	Sample standard deviation	N	Sample mean	Sample standard deviation
Respondents	299	0.150	0.982	312	1.857	2.236
Nonrespondents	101	−0.591	0.835	88	0.724	0.571
Total	400	−0.037	1.000	400	1.608	2.047
Population values	—	0.0	1.0	—	1.649	2.161

[a] Normal data Y are sampled from the normal $(0, 1)$ distribution; lognormal data are the exponential of the normal values. Response is determined by a logistic response function

$$\Pr(R = 1 \mid Y) = \exp(\alpha_0 + \alpha_1 Y)\big/\big[1 + \exp(\alpha_0 + \alpha_1 Y)\big],$$

where $(\alpha_0, \alpha_1) = (1, 1)$ for normal data and $(0, 1)$ for lognormal data.

Table 2. Maximum likelihood estimates of coefficients for logistic response functions assuming all data in Table 1 are observed[a]

Coefficient	Normal data		Lognormal data	
	Estimate	Standard error	Estimate	Standard error
α_0	1.28	0.134	0.225	0.206
α_1	0.856	0.140	0.995	0.205

[a] Model: response R satisfies $\Pr(R = 1 \mid Y) = \exp(\alpha_0 + \alpha_1 Y)/[1 + \exp(\alpha_0 + \alpha_1 Y)]$

is $\exp(0.5) = 1.6487$, and its theoretical variance is $e(e-1) = 4.6708$. The estimates for the response function are the maximum likelihood estimates from logistic regression assuming all Y values are available. Standard errors are estimated by the second derivatives of the log likelihood evaluated at the maximum likelihood estimates. From Tables 1 and 2 it is clear that the generated data are typical of the distributions from which they were drawn.

We performed another simulation to examine the effect of having a variable X related to Y but independent of response given Y; or a variable X related to response but independent of Y (see Section VI). Two samples, each with 400 units and denoted by X_i and Y_i, were independently generated from the normal distribution with mean zero and variance one. Another 400 values, denoted by U_i, were randomly generated from the uniform distribution on the interval $(0, 1)$. All data were generated using the random function generators in the SAS statistical package (SAS Institute, 1982). Two data sets with some nonresponse were generated as follows. For the first, Y was considered the outcome, and response was a logistic function of X and Y. Specifically, for each i, define R_i to be one (respondent) if

$$\exp(1 + Y_i + X_i)\big/\big[1 + \exp(1 + Y_i + X_i)\big] \geq U_i,$$

and to be zero otherwise (nonrespondent). For the second, define $Y_i' = X_i + Y_i$ and consider Y_i' to be the outcome variable. Respondents in this data set are defined to be those units with

$$\exp(1 + Y_i')\big/\big[1 + \exp(1 + Y_i')\big] \geq U_i.$$

Thus, the response function for this second data set is identical to the response function R_i in the first data set. The first data set has the theoretical properties that Y is independent of X, but response depends on X. In the second data set Y' is linearly dependent on X, but, conditional on Y', R is independent of X.

Table 3 shows sample estimates of parameters of the distributions of these two generated data sets. Table 4 shows maximum likelihood estimates of the parameters of the nonresponse function assuming all values of the outcome variables are observed. Because the logistic coefficient of the

Table 3. Sample moments of generated data with a covariate[a]

	N	Covariate X Sample mean	Covariate X Sample standard deviation	Outcome Y Sample mean	Outcome Y Sample standard deviation	Outcome Y' Sample mean	Outcome Y' Sample standard deviation
Respondents	272	0.271	1.021	0.309	0.952	0.580	1.311
Nonrespondents	128	−0.389	0.922	−0.541	0.860	−0.930	1.196
Total	400	0.060	1.036	0.037	1.005	0.097	1.456

[a] X and Y are independently sampled from the normal distribution with mean 0 and variance 1; $Y' = X + Y$; Response is generated by a logistic response function

$$\Pr(R = 1 \mid X, Y) = \exp(1 + Y')/[1 + \exp(1 + Y')]$$

outcome variables in the response function is positive, levels of the outcome variables for the respondents are generally larger than those of the nonrespondents.

Further evaluation of the selection model and mixture model approaches used data from a mailed survey of alcohol consumption behaviors sent to a population of men of retirement age. Level of alcohol consumption or problems with drinking may be related to participation rates in population surveys (Bergstrand et al., 1983). In September 1982 participants in the Normative Aging Study were asked to fill out a mailed drinking question-

Table 4. Maximum likelihood estimates of parameters of the logistic response function for data in Table 3 assuming nonrespondents' data were observed

Model 1[a]		
Coefficient	Estimate	Standard error
α_0	0.969	0.134
α_1	1.153	0.152
α_2	0.879	0.143

Model 2[b]		
Coefficient	Estimate	Standard error
α_0	0.963	0.133
α_1	1.011	0.118

[a] Outcome is Y and response function is

$$\Pr(R = 1 \mid X, Y) = \exp(\alpha_0 + \alpha_1 Y + \alpha_2 X)/[1 + \exp(\alpha_0 + \alpha_1 Y + \alpha_2 X)].$$

[b] Outcome is Y' and response function is

$$\Pr(R = 1 \mid X, Y) = \exp(\alpha_0 + \alpha_1 Y')/[1 + \exp(\alpha_0 + \alpha_1 Y')]$$

naire inquiring about their quantity, frequency, and variability of alcohol consumption, problems with drinking, and their contexts and motives for drinking (Glynn et al., 1985). The Normative Aging Study is a longitudinal study of 2000 community-dwelling men being conducted by the Veterans Administration in Boston (Bossé et al., 1984). Since being recruited in the 1960s, participants have reported for physical examinations every 3 to 5 years and have been asked to fill out questionnaires about smoking, work and retirement attitudes, and drinking habits. For the current example, considering the relationship of retirement status to average alcohol consumption, we restrict attention to the 1423 active participants in the Normative Aging Study who were between 50 and 69 years old in 1982. Thirty-eight of the nonrespondents to this 1982 questionnaire were subsequently interviewed about their drinking behaviors and can be considered follow-ups. The analyses presented are intended only to illustrate methods of adjusting for suspected nonignorable nonresponse. They are not intended to provide a definitive analysis of the relationship of retirement to drinking behaviors. Such an analysis would require attention to residuals, consideration of potential confounding variables such as circumstances of retirement and the health status of respondents, and consideration of other outcomes such as the frequency of drinking occasions and drinking problems.

Table 5 shows the numbers of respondents to the 1982 Normative Aging Study drinking questionnaire within each of four birth cohorts. Of the 151 nonrespondents, retirement status was subsequently determined for 112 men. These 112 men either responded to one of two postcards asking only about their retirement status and date of retirement, filled out a detailed questionnaire about their work and retirement attitudes, filled out a mailed personality questionnaire including a work status question, or reported for

Table 5. Numbers of respondents to the 1982 Normative Aging Study drinking questionnaire within birth cohorts

Birth year	Number mailed the 1982 questionnaire	Number with retirement status determined	Number of respondents	Number of interviewed nonrespondents
1928–1932 (aged 50–54)	407	390	329	17
1923–1927 (aged 55–59)	430	419	398	5
1918–1922 (aged 60–64)	361	354	334	10
1913–1917 (aged 65–69)	225	221	211	6
Total	1423	1384	1272	38

a subsequent physical examination at which their work status in 1982 was determined. The 39 men born between 1913 and 1932 who did not respond to the drinking questionnaire and whose retirement status in 1982 could not be determined were excluded from subsequent analyses. This is primarily done to simplify the illustration of techniques requiring complete information on predictor variables. However, it is also arguable that the nonresponse of these 39 men is not related to drinking since they also have not responded to other questionnaires from the Normative Aging Study.

From July 11, 1983, to March 6, 1985, an interview about drinking behaviors was included in Normative Aging Study physical examinations. During this interval 584 of the 1384 men in the population for this analysis reported for physical examinations and all but four of these men were interviewed. These four men all answered the 1982 questionnaire. Reasons for failure to interview were absence of a qualified interviewer (two missed interviews) or press of time on the part of the participant (two missed interviews). Of the 580 interviewed men, 38 were nonrespondents to the 1982 questionnaire. These 38 men will be considered follow-ups in the analysis of the relationship of retirement to average alcohol consumption level. Follow-ups were classified according to their work status at the time of their interview; the remaining 1346 men were classified according to their work status in September 1982. As is common for follow-up data from sample surveys, the follow-ups are not exactly a random sample of the nonrespondents and their data were not collected in a manner identical to the data of the respondents (interview versus mailed questionnaire). We will, however, ignore these complications.

The outcome variable for the current analysis is a natural log transform of current average alcohol consumption. The transform is made because it has been argued that for a wide variety of populations the distribution of average daily consumption among alcohol consumers is approximately lognormal (de Lint and Schmidt, 1976). About 15% of respondents to the 1982 questionnaire were nondrinkers so the overall distribution is theoreti-

Table 6. Mean alcohol consumption level and retirement status within response group and birth cohort[a]

		Respondents			Nonrespondents		
Birth year	N	Percent retired	Mean ($\pm$ s.d.) log(1 + drinks/day)	N	Percent retired	Number interviewed	Interview Mean ($\pm$ s.d.) log(1 + drinks/day)
1928–1932	329	7.6	0.79 ($\pm$0.57)	61	8.2	17	0.52 ($\pm$0.42)
1922–1927	398	21.6	0.69 ($\pm$0.57)	21	9.5	5	0.56 ($\pm$0.61)
1918–1922	334	43.4	0.71 ($\pm$0.58)	20	25.0	10	0.84 ($\pm$0.64)
1913–1917	211	79.1	0.64 ($\pm$0.54)	10	100.0	6	0.86 ($\pm$0.82)

[a] Data from Table 5.

cally a mixture of a lognormal distribution with a group of values identically zero. Table 6 shows mean levels of log(1 + drinks/day) within response groups and birth cohorts. Sample moments for nonrespondents are based on data from the 38 follow-ups. Among respondents there is a tendency for men from older cohorts to report lower average consumption levels compared to men in younger cohorts. This is consistent with data from other cross-sectional surveys (Clark and Midanik, 1982). Although the sample is small, the trend among the follow-ups was for men from older cohorts to report higher average consumption levels, compared to follow-ups from younger cohorts.

Summaries of ordinary least squares regressions of log(1 + drinks/day) on retirement status, birth year, and retirement status times birth year for respondents and follow-ups are shown in Table 7. Coefficients for respondents can be interpreted as follows: working men from older cohorts reported drinking slightly less than working men in younger cohorts; there were no cohort differences in consumption levels among retirees; and retirees in older cohorts were drinking slightly more than older workers, but younger retirees were drinking about the same amounts as younger workers. From such cross-sectional data, it is impossible to determine whether older retirees have increased their drinking or lighter drinkers are more likely to remain in the work force. Although estimated standard errors are large, estimated coefficients for all three predictors of log(1 + drinks/day) have the opposite sign among the follow-ups than they do among the respondents.

Table 7. Summary of ordinary least squares estimates of the regression of log(1 + drinks/day) on retirement status (0 = working, 1 = retired), birth year, and retirement status × birth year interaction[a]

	Estimates based on 1272 respondents to the 1982 questionnaire		Estimates based on 38 nonrespondents from whom log(1 + drink/day) was later obtained	
Variable	Coefficient	Standard error	Coefficient	Standard error
Retirement status	0.334	0.166	−0.589	0.900
Birth year	0.0144	0.00434	−0.0292	0.0252
Retirement × birth year	−0.0141	0.00747	0.0372	0.0385
Intercept	0.00161	0.0159	−0.0280	0.0948
	R-square = 0.0091		R-square = 0.122	
	Root mean square error = 0.568		Root mean square error = 0.565	

[a]All variables are mean centered.

IV. Simulation with No Covariates

The simplest version of the selection model has no covariates and no predictors of response, other than Y itself. In this case (using the logistic response model of Greenlees et al., 1982),

$$Y_i = \beta_0 + \epsilon_i \quad \text{and}$$

$$P(R_i = 1 | Y_i) = \exp(\alpha_0 + \alpha_1 Y) / [1 + \exp(\alpha_0 + \alpha_1 Y)].$$

Estimates of the parameters β_0, σ, α_0, and α_1 for the data in Table 1 were obtained using the selection model approach considering only the respondents' data to be known. Each respondent's contribution to the log likelihood was

$$l_i = -\log(2\pi\sigma^2)/2 - (Y_i - \beta_0)^2/2\sigma^2 + \alpha_0 + \alpha_1 Y_i$$
$$- \log[1 + \exp(\alpha_0 + \alpha_1 Y_i)].$$

Each nonrespondent's contribution to the log likelihood was

$$l_{nr} = \log \left\{ \int \Phi[(Y - \beta_0)/\sigma] \Big/ \{\sigma[1 + \exp(\alpha_0 + \alpha_1 Y)]\} \, dY \right\}.$$

Estimating the integral by ten point Gauss–Hermite quadrature yields

$$l_{nr} \approx \log \left[\sum_{j=1}^{10} A_j \Big/ \{\sqrt{\pi}[1 + \exp(\alpha_0 + \sqrt{2}\sigma\alpha_1 R_j + \alpha_1\beta_0)]\} \right],$$

where A_j are the coefficients and R_j are the roots of the tenth degree Hermite polynomial.

Results of constrained maximizations of the log likelihood of the normal data from Table 1 based on the BMDP programs are shown in Table 8. All parameters began with initial estimates derived from the values of the respondents; namely $\hat{\beta}_0 = 0.15$, $\hat{\sigma} = 0.98$, and $\hat{\alpha}_0 = 2.0$. Unless otherwise constrained, the initial estimate of α_1 was 0. When α_1 was not fixed, the method requiring analytic specification of derivatives and the method not requiring such specification found similar minimum values for $-\log$ likelihood and fairly similar parameter estimates. Estimates of β_0 and σ from these approaches were closer to the population values than estimates based on the sample moments of the respondents only. Estimates of α_0 and α_1 were also fairly reasonable given population values. Both of these approaches produced very large estimates of standard errors of parameters based on the second derivatives of the log likelihood. Considering minimum values of the $-\log$ likelihood obtainable when α_1 was fixed, it appears that the likelihood is fairly flat near its maximum. Asymptotic estimates of standard errors are probably unreliable because it does not appear that the log likelihood is nearly quadratic. When α_1 was fixed, much smaller estimated standard errors were obtained.

Table 8. Joint maximum likelihood estimates[a,b]

Constraints	Method	$-$Log likelihood	$\hat{\beta}_0$	$\hat{\sigma}$	$\hat{\alpha}_0$	$\hat{\alpha}_1$
$-10 \le \beta_0 \le 10, 0 \le \sigma \le 10,$	Derivatives	644.405	0.065	0.99	1.09	0.34
$-5 \le \alpha_0 \le 5, -3 \le \alpha_1 \le 3$	unspecified		(± 1.00)[c]	(± 0.28)	(± 0.98)	(± 4.07)
$-10 \le \beta_0 \le 10, 0 \le \sigma \le 10,$	Derivatives	644.409	0.096	0.98	1.07	0.21
$-5 \le \alpha_0 \le 5, -3 \le \alpha_1 \le 3$	specified		(± 3.38)	(± 0.52)	(± 0.76)	(± 14.00)
$\alpha_1 \equiv 0$	Derivatives	644.402	0.15	0.98	1.09	0.00
	unspecified		(± 0.057)	(± 0.040)	(± 0.12)	(± 0.00)
$\alpha_1 \equiv 2$	Derivatives	646.877	-0.25	1.17	2.45	2.00
	specified		(± 0.065)	(± 0.060)	(± 0.17)	(± 0.00)
$\alpha_1 \equiv 0.1$	Derivatives	644.402	0.12	0.98	1.08	0.10
	unspecified		(± 0.057)	(± 0.040)	(± 0.12)	(± 0.00)

[a] Model: $Y \simeq N(\beta_0, \sigma^2)$

$$Pr(R = 1 \mid Y) = \exp(\alpha_0 + \alpha_1 Y)/[1 + \exp(\alpha_0 + \alpha_1 Y)].$$

Data: R for the normal data in Table 1 and normal values for respondents.

[b] Each respondent's contribution to the log likelihood was

$$l_i = -\log(2\pi\sigma^2)/2 - (Y_i - \beta_0)^2/2\sigma^2 + \alpha_0 + \alpha_1 Y_i - \log[1 + \exp(\alpha_0 + \alpha_1 Y_i)].$$

Each nonrespondent's contribution to log likelihood was

$$l_{nr} = \log\left\{ \int \Phi[(Y - \beta_0)/\sigma] \Big/ \{\sigma[1 + \exp(\alpha_0 + \alpha_1 Y)]\} \, dY \right\}.$$

[c] Estimated standard errors of parameters are shown in parentheses; these are based on approximate second derivatives of the log likelihood at the maximum likelihood estimates.

The program ZXMWD from the International Mathematical and Statistical Libraries (IMSL) (1982) subroutines was also used to maximize the log likelihood of the normal data. Constraints were $-10 \le \beta_0 \le 10$; $0.01 \le \sigma \le 10.0$; $-5 \le \alpha_0 \le 5$; and $-3 \le \alpha_1 \le 3$. The program was allowed to execute for 1.52 minutes at a cost of \$38.14. It performed 743 iterations but did not converge. At each iteration parameter estimates and values of the log likelihood were printed. The largest observed value of $-$log likelihood was 3787.76 occurring at $\hat{\beta}_0 = 0.2686$, $\hat{\sigma} = 2.507$, $\hat{\alpha}_0 = -2.5000$, and $\hat{\alpha}_1 = -1.5000$. The smallest observed value of $-$log likelihood was 644.398 occurring at $\hat{\beta}_0 = 0.2689$, $\hat{\sigma} = 1.0010$, $\hat{\alpha}_0 = 1.2740$, and $\hat{\alpha}_1 = -0.4905$. This value of $-$log likelihood is slightly smaller than the minimum found by the BMDP programs.

To investigate the dependence of the BMDP maximization programs on starting values, the derivatives-unspecified program in BMDP was used to maximize the log likelihood with starting values equal to the values which produced the maximum log likelihood according to the IMSL program. Convergence was not met in 50 iterations. Shown in Table 9 are 35 different sets of parameter values which produced virtually identical values of the log

Table 9. Thirty-five different sets of parameter values producing virtually identical values of the log likelihood of the normal data and their associated logistic response function[a]

− Log likelihood	$\hat{\beta}_0$	$\hat{\sigma}$	$\hat{\alpha}_0$	$\hat{\alpha}_1$
644.398	0.27	1.00	1.27	− 0.49
644.404	0.24	0.99	1.20	− 0.38
644.422	0.22	0.98	1.14	− 0.28
644.424	0.21	0.99	1.17	− 0.25
644.402	0.23	0.99	1.20	− 0.33
644.404	0.25	0.99	1.22	− 0.41
644.453	0.27	1.00	1.24	− 0.50
644.415	0.24	0.99	1.18	− 0.34
644.415	0.20	0.98	1.11	− 0.17
644.402	0.17	0.98	1.10	− 0.07
644.403	0.19	0.99	1.13	− 0.16
644.436	0.21	0.99	1.18	− 0.25
644.416	0.13	0.98	1.08	0.10
644.428	0.15	0.98	1.11	− 0.00
644.424	0.25	0.99	1.23	− 0.38
644.442	0.22	0.99	1.19	− 0.27
644.426	0.18	0.98	1.13	− 0.10
644.416	0.16	0.98	1.09	− 0.00
644.418	0.12	0.98	1.08	0.18
644.420	0.09	0.99	1.09	0.27
644.440	0.11	0.98	1.05	0.19
644.455	0.09	0.98	1.05	0.28
644.454	0.13	0.98	1.06	0.15
644.442	0.16	0.98	1.08	0.04
644.438	0.13	0.98	1.07	0.16
644.440	0.15	0.98	1.07	0.06
644.437	0.11	0.99	1.08	0.24
644.441	0.13	0.98	1.09	0.16
644.430	0.17	0.98	1.09	− 0.02
644.444	0.19	0.98	1.13	− 0.11
644.434	0.15	0.98	1.09	0.07
644.436	0.12	0.98	1.07	0.16
644.443	0.20	0.98	1.14	− 0.16
644.436	0.16	0.98	1.08	0.02
644.449	0.07	1.00	1.12	0.41

[a]Values of the log likelihood are close to the maximum in Table 8.

Table 10. Joint maximum likelihood estimates[a]

Constraints	Method	$-$Log likelihood	$\hat{\beta}_0$	$\hat{\sigma}$	$\hat{\alpha}_0$	$\hat{\alpha}_1$
$-10 \leq \beta_0 \leq 10, 0 \leq \sigma \leq 10,$ $-5 \leq \alpha_0 \leq 7, -5 \leq \alpha_1 \leq 5$	Derivatives specified	805.587	0.83 (± 0.18)[b]	2.68 (± 0.064)	0.65 (± 0.86)	5.00[c]
$-10 \leq \beta_0 \leq 10, 0 \leq \sigma \leq 10,$ $-5 \leq \alpha_0 \leq 7, -5 \leq \alpha_1 \leq 5$	Derivatives unspecified	805.654	0.84[d]	2.67[d]	0.56[d]	5.00[d]
$\alpha_1 \equiv 0$	Derivatives unspecified	904.018	1.86 (± 0.22)	2.23 (± 0.062)	1.26 (± 0.12)	0.00 (± 0.00)
$\alpha_1 \equiv 1$	Derivatives unspecified	871.673	1.10 (± 0.24)	2.56 (± 0.072)	0.93 (± 0.30)	1.00 (± 0.00)
$\alpha_1 \equiv 4$	Derivatives specified	813.769	0.79 (± 0.19)	2.72 (± 0.067)	0.73 (± 0.75)	4.00 (± 0.00)

[a] Model: $Y \simeq N(\beta_0, \sigma^2)$

$$\Pr(R = 1 \mid Y) = \exp(\alpha_0 + \alpha_1 Y)/[1 + \exp(\alpha_0 + \alpha_1 Y)].$$

Data: R for the lognormal data in Table 1 and lognormal values for respondents.

[b] Estimated standard errors of parameters are shown in parentheses.

[c] Maximum occurred with α_1 on the boundary; other standard errors are calculated with α_1 fixed at this boundary value.

[d] Standard errors could not be estimated in this model because convergence could not be attained.

likelihood. These are the 35 smallest values of $-$log likelihood that the BMDP program found as it searched for a maximum of the log likelihood. Results indicate that there are a wide range of values in the parameter space that produce nearly identical values of the log likelihood.

Table 10 shows results of constrained maximizations of the log likelihood of the lognormal data summarized in Table 1. Initial parameter estimates were $\hat{\beta}_0 = 1.9$, $\hat{\sigma} = 2.2$, and $\hat{\alpha}_0 = 3.0$. Unless otherwise constrained, the initial estimate of α_1 was 0. When α_1 was constrained to be between -5 and 5, the smallest values of $-$log likelihood were found to lie on the boundary with $\alpha_1 = 5$, and therefore it was not possible to obtain an estimated standard error based on standard asymptotic arguments. Even after 75 iterations the derivative free approach with α_1 not fixed did not converge and thus no estimated standard errors were obtained. No smaller value of $-$log likelihood could be obtained with α_1 fixed at 0, 1, or 4. Wider intervals for α_0 and α_1 were considered, but the programs then failed because of overflow and underflow problems.

These programs generally produced large underestimates of β_0 for the lognormal data. The exception occurred when α_1 was fixed at zero, in which case nonresponse is ignorable and the estimate of β_0 is the respondents' mean. The parameter α_1 which indexes the relationship between level of Y and response also could not be reliably estimated. This example demonstrates the sensitivity of this approach to the assumption that Y has a normal distribution.

V. Simulation with One Covariate X

In contrast to the above results, Greenlees et al. (1982) obtained relatively much smaller estimated standard errors for the parameters in their model. A fundamental difference between the above simulation and their example was that their example contained some covariates X predictive of Y but conditionally given Y unrelated to response, and other covariates Z predictive of response but conditionally independent of Y.

The selection model approach was used to estimate the parameters of the distributions of the outcome variables as well as the parameters of the response functions for both data sets summarized in Table 3. We assumed that values of X were available for all units, but values of the outcome variables were only available for respondents. Correctly specified models were also assumed; i.e., it was assumed that Y was independent of X and that response depended upon Y and X; also that Y' was a linear function of X, but, conditional on Y', response was independent of X. Results are shown in Table 11. For both data sets very good estimates of all parameters

Table 11. Jointly estimated maximum likelihood estimates of parameters of the linear regression and the logistic response function using respondents' data and R from Table 3

Model 1[a]							
Constraints	Method	$-$Log likelihood	$\hat{\beta}_0$	$\hat{\sigma}$	$\hat{\alpha}_0$	$\hat{\alpha}_1$	$\hat{\alpha}_2$
$-10 \le \beta_0 \le 10, 0 \le \sigma \le 10,$ $-5 \le \alpha_i \le 5, i = 0,1,2$	Derivatives unspecified	600.40	-0.022 (± 0.12)	1.05 (± 0.09)	1.12 (± 0.37)	1.38 (± 0.49)	0.99 (± 0.20)
$-10 \le \beta_0 \le 10, 0 \le \sigma \le 10,$ $-5 \le \alpha_i \le 5, i = 0,1,2$	Derivatives specified	600.39	-0.013 (± 0.12)	1.05 (± 0.09)	1.10 (± 0.38)	1.35 (± 0.49)	0.98 (± 0.21)

[a] $Y \mid X \simeq \text{normal}(\beta_0, \sigma^2)$ and the response function is

$$\Pr(R = 1 \mid X, Y) = \exp(\alpha_0 + \alpha_1 Y + \alpha_2 X)/[1 + \exp(\alpha_0 + \alpha_1 Y + \alpha_2 X)].$$

Model 2[b]						
Constraints	Method	$-$Log likelihood	$\hat{\beta}_0$	$\hat{\beta}_1$	$\hat{\sigma}$	$\hat{\alpha}_0$	$\hat{\alpha}_1$
$-10 \le \beta_i \le 10, i = 0,1,$ $0 \le \sigma \le 10, -5 \le \alpha_i \le 5,$ $i = 0,1$	Derivatives unspecified	600.87	0.085 (± 0.071)	0.98 (± 0.05)	1.01 (± 0.05)	0.86 (± 0.17)	0.90 (± 0.18)
$-10 \le \beta_i \le 10, i = 0,1,$ $0 \le \sigma \le 10, -5 \le \alpha_i \le 5,$ $i = 0,1$	Derivatives specified	600.86	0.091 (± 0.074)	0.98 (± 0.06)	1.00 (± 0.06)	0.86 (± 0.15)	0.89 (± 0.17)

[b] $Y' \mid X \simeq \text{normal}(\beta_0 + \beta_1 X, \sigma^2)$ and the response function is

$$\Pr(R = 1 \mid X, Y') = \exp(\alpha_0 + \alpha_1 Y')/[1 + \exp(\alpha_0 + \alpha_1 Y')]$$

were obtained. In particular, estimates of the linear regression parameters were much better than estimates based on respondents only. This approach also produced very reasonable estimates of standard errors.

These results indicate that the selection model can perform well when there is a covariate X predictive of response, which is either conditionally unrelated to the outcome or predictive of outcome but conditionally unrelated to response. Such a covariate X is virtually never known in actual practice. Also, the selection model is sensitive to the correct specification of predictors of outcome and response. To illustrate the problem of a misspecified model, we obtained maximum likelihood estimates of parameters in the selection model, assuming for the data in Table 3 that Y has a regression on X and response is a logistic function of Y. The estimated regression intercept ($\pm$ S.E.) was 0.864 ($\pm$0.132), and the estimated slope on X was -0.344 ($\pm$0.092). Parameters in another misspecified model were also estimated. Assuming response depends on Y' and X, the estimated mean ($\pm$ S.E.) of Y' from the selection model assuming Y' and X are uncorrelated was 1.20 ($\pm$0.11). Estimation under a misspecified selection model can produce very biased answers.

VI. Extension When a Sample of Nonrespondents' Data Is Obtained

The above findings are not generally encouraging about the selection model. One natural way to improve this approach is to obtain some Y values for the nonrespondents. This might happen, for example, if a subsample of the nonrespondents were intensively pursued and their Y values obtained. Units in this subsample are called follow-ups. It is also possible, for modeling purposes, to consider late respondents to a mailed survey to be followed up nonrespondents. If some Y values for nonrespondents are obtainable, models for nonresponse may be far more robust.

The performance of this extended approach can be illustrated using the generated data without a covariate described in Tables 1 and 2. Assume that a subsample of follow-ups is obtained. The contribution to the log likelihood for such a follow-up is

$$l_i = -\log(2\pi\sigma^2)/2 - (Y_i - \beta_0)^2/2\sigma^2 - \log[1 + \exp(\alpha_0 + \alpha_1 Y_i)].$$

Maximum likelihood estimates of the parameters of the normal data, assuming varying numbers of follow-ups, are shown in Table 12. The nonlinear regression programs in BMDP were used to obtain these estimates. The four different estimates of the parameters were obtained by assuming that there were no unobserved Y values among the first 40 individuals, the first 80 individuals, the first 100 individuals, and any of the 400 individuals.

Table 12. Joint maximum likelihood estimates under the model in Table 8 extended to allow for "observed" nonrespondents[a,b]

Number of "observed" nonrespondents	− Log likelihood	$\hat{\beta}_0$	$\hat{\sigma}$	$\hat{\alpha}_0$	$\hat{\alpha}_1$
11	657.730	− 0.009	1.012	1.197	0.677
		$(\pm 0.099)^c$	(± 0.057)	(± 0.213)	(± 0.381)
24	671.510	− 0.029	1.008	1.248	0.782
		(± 0.079)	(± 0.051)	(± 0.200)	(± 0.296)
28	676.162	− 0.008	0.997	1.210	0.689
		(± 0.075)	(± 0.047)	(± 0.171)	(± 0.276)
101	770.559	− 0.037	0.998	1.281	0.856
		(± 0.050)	(± 0.037)	(± 0.137)	(± 0.139)

[a] Model: $Y \simeq N(\beta_0, \sigma^2)$

$$\Pr(R = 1 \mid Y) = \exp(\alpha_0 + \alpha_1 Y)/[1 + \exp(\alpha_0 + \alpha_1 Y)].$$

Data: R for the normal data in Table 1, respondents' normal data, and randomly chosen "observed" nonrespondents' normal data from Table 1.

[b] Each "observed" nonrespondent's contribution to the log likelihood was

$$l_i = -\log(2\pi\sigma^2)/2 - (Y_i - \beta_0)^2/2\sigma^2 - \log[1 + \exp(\alpha_0 + \alpha_1 Y_i)].$$

[c] Estimated standard errors of parameters are shown in parentheses.

Notice that the values obtained by this approach assuming all Y values are observed are virtually identical to the parameter estimates and standard errors displayed in Tables 1 and 2. Even when there are only 11 follow-ups, this approach performs well. The estimated mean of Y is closer to the true mean than the estimate based on respondents only. Reasonable estimates for the parameters of nonresponse are also obtained with only a small percentage of nonrespondents' values observed. Estimated standard errors of parameters from this approach are much smaller than those displayed in Table 8.

Maximum likelihood estimates of the parameters of the lognormal data, assuming that varying numbers of follow-ups are obtained, are shown in Table 13. The nonlinear regression programs in BMDP were used to obtain these estimates. The six different estimates of the parameters were obtained by assuming that there were no unobserved Y values among the first 40 individuals, the first 80 individuals, the first 100 individuals, the first 200 individuals, the first 300 individuals, and any of the 400 individuals. When few follow-ups are obtained, these maximum likelihood estimates of the mean are smaller than their population values. Estimates of the standard deviation and the nonresponse parameters are larger than their population values. These deviations from population values persisted even when more than half of the nonrespondents were followed up. The selection model

Table 13. Joint maximum likelihood estimates under the model in Table 10 extended to allow for "observed" nonrespondents[a]

Number of "observed" nonrespondents	− Log likelihood	$\hat{\beta}_0$	$\hat{\sigma}$	$\hat{\alpha}_0$	$\hat{\alpha}_1$
9	845.66	0.934	2.536	−0.167	5.00
		(± 0.146)[b]	(± 0.050)	(± 0.295)	(± 0.00)[c]
21	895.57	1.030	2.478	−0.434	3.982
		(± 0.154)	(± 0.050)	(± 0.308)	(± 0.408)
25	914.45	1.054	2.460	−0.283	3.137
		(± 0.157)	(± 0.050)	(± 0.283)	(± 0.334)
46	968.91	1.436	2.209	0.243	1.309
		(± 0.175)	(± 0.046)	(± 0.244)	(± 0.255)
72	1013.06	1.556	2.085	0.171	1.169
		(± 0.175)	(± 0.042)	(± 0.219)	(± 0.231)
88	1041.42	1.605	2.029	0.225	0.995
		(± 0.175)	(± 0.041)	(± 0.208)	(± 0.207)

[a] Model: $Y \simeq N(\beta_0, \sigma^2)$

$$Pr(R = 1 \mid Y) = \exp(\alpha_0 + \alpha_1 Y)/[1 + \exp(\alpha_0 + \alpha_1 Y)].$$

Data: R for the lognormal data in Table 1, respondents' lognormal data, and randomly chosen "observed" nonrespondents' lognormal data from Table 1.

[b] Estimated standard errors of parameters are shown in parentheses.

[c] Maximum occurs with α_1 on the boundary; other standard errors are calculated with α_1 fixed at the boundary value.

approach tries to make the distribution of Y symmetric, and thus systematically underestimates the values of the unobserved Y values.

If the goal of analysis is to obtain unbiased estimates of regression parameters, then this modified version of the selection model approach offers only limited promise. The approach does not appear to be robust against departures from normality and is not recommended unless there is confidence that the residuals from the regression really are normally distributed.

VII. Mixture Model Approach

Means of the data in Table 1 assuming some follow-ups are available were also estimated using a mixture model approach. Table 14 shows mixture model estimates of the mean of the normally distributed data described in Tables 1 and 2. When a noninformative prior was chosen for the nonrespondents' mean, the posterior overall mean is a weighted sum of the sample mean of the respondents and the sample mean of the nonrespon-

Table 14. Mixture model estimates of parameters assuming the prior distribution of the nonrespondents is normal[a]

	Prior = $N(0, \infty)$		Prior = $N(-0.3, 0.09)$	
Number of follow-ups	Sample mean ($\pm$ S.E.) of follow-ups	Posterior overall mean ($\pm$ S.E.)	Posterior mean ($\pm$ S.E.) of nonrespondents	Posterior overall mean ($\pm$ S.E.)
11	−0.49 (±0.25)	−0.010 (±0.077)	−0.41 (±0.19)	0.008 (±0.065)
24	−0.54 (±0.14)	−0.025 (±0.058)	−0.50 (±0.13)	−0.014 (±0.055)
28	−0.47 (±0.13)	−0.006 (±0.056)	−0.44 (±0.12)	0.001 (±0.054)
101	−0.59 (±0.08)	−0.037 (±0.050)	−0.57 (±0.08)	−0.032 (±0.050)

[a] Normal data from Table 1.

dents. The prior mean and standard deviation for the nonrespondents of −0.3 and 0.3, respectively, were arbitrarily chosen. These estimates should be compared to the estimates based on the selection model which are shown in Table 12. Estimates of the overall mean are fairly comparable in the two approaches, but the selection model performs slightly better. Both approaches perform better the greater the number of follow-ups.

Table 15 shows mixture model estimates of the mean of the lognormally distributed data described in Tables 1 and 2. Here it is wrongly assumed that both respondents and nonrespondents are sampled from normal distributions. The prior mean and standard deviation for the nonrespondents of 0.3 and 0.3, respectively, were arbitrarily chosen; with only a small number of followups the posterior mean for the nonrespondents is dominated by these observed values. Compared to the selection model approach (Table 13), the mixture model approach produces much better estimates in this case. The mixture model approach also outperforms the estimated mean based on respondents only. This gives evidence that the mixture model approach is more robust to departures from the assumed underlying distri-

Table 15. Mixture model estimates of parameters assuming the prior distribution of the nonrespondents is normal[a]

	Prior = $N(0, \infty)$		Prior = $N(0.3, 0.09)$	
Number of follow-ups	Sample mean ($\pm$ S.E.) of follow-ups	Posterior overall mean ($\pm$ S.E.)	Posterior mean ($\pm$ S.E.) of nonrespondents	Posterior overall mean ($\pm$ S.E.)
9	0.61 (±0.10)	1.58 (±0.10)	0.58 (±0.09)	1.58 (±0.10)
21	0.67 (±0.11)	1.60 (±0.11)	0.63 (±0.10)	1.59 (±0.10)
25	0.75 (±0.11)	1.61 (±0.10)	0.69 (±0.11)	1.60 (±0.10)
88	0.72 (±0.05)	1.61 (±0.10)	0.71 (±0.06)	1.60 (±0.10)

[a] Lognormal data from Table 1.

bution. Since it also performs well when distributional assumptions are correct, the mixture model approach is the recommended procedure for mean estimation with nonignorable missingness.

VIII. Application to Drinking Data

To illustrate the selection model and mixture model approaches in a setting where it is suspected that response is related to the outcome, we analyzed data from a survey of drinking behaviors. It was suspected that heavier drinkers would be less likely to respond to a mailed drinking survey. Data were summarized in Tables 5 to 7.

Linear regression coefficients in the entire population were estimated using the selection model approach assuming nonresponse has a logistic functional form. Results are summarized in Tables 16 and 17. All models were fit using the function maximization routine in BMDP requiring the analytical specification of derivatives (Dixon, 1981). This approach con-

Table 16. Joint maximum likelihood estimates of the linear regression of log(1 + drinks/day) on retirement status, birth year, and retirement status × birth year interaction and the logistic regression of response on log(1 + drinks/day) and birth year[a]

	Parameters of linear regression			
	Without follow-ups		With follow-ups	
Variable	Coefficient	Standard error	Coefficient	Standard error
Retirement status	0.165	0.180	0.295	0.165
Birth year	0.00651	0.00474	0.0124	0.00442
Retirement × birth year	−0.00572	0.00801	−0.0120	0.00733
Intercept	−0.0864	0.0178	−0.00345	0.0180
Root mean	0.630	0.0146	0.568	0.0145
square error				
	Parameters of logistic response			
Log(1 + drinks/day)	6.00	[b]	0.176	0.290
Birth year	−0.109	0.0349	−0.096	0.018
Intercept	6.00	[b]	2.539	0.106
	−log likelihood = 1414.08		−log likelihood = 1493.82	

[a] Parameters are constrained to lie between −6 and 6.

[b] Maximum occurred with these parameters on the boundary; other standard errors are calculated with these parameters fixed at these boundary values.

verged more rapidly and was far cheaper than the BMDP maximization routine not requiring derivatives to be specified. Models summarized in Table 16 assumed that the probability of response to the questionnaire was a logistic function of log(1 + drinks/day) and birth year, whereas those in Table 17 assumed the logistic response function depended on log(1 + drinks/day) and retirement status. These two methods were considered because the experience described in Section V illustrated that the selection model approach produces better estimates when there is a covariate related to outcome but not to response. There is no evidence to support either of these two models. For each of the assumed functional forms for response, two estimations were made—one ignored the follow-ups and the other accounted for them, as described in Section V.

Comparing the estimated linear regression coefficients in Table 16 with those in Table 17 reveals some large differences. Assuming response depends on both log(1 + drinks/day) and retirement status but not birth year yields an estimated main effect of birth year more than two standard errors greater than the estimated effect of birth year assuming that response depends on log(1 + drinks/day) and birth year but not retirement status. All three of the estimated linear regression coefficients of the predictor

Table 17. Joint maximum likelihood estimates of the linear regression of log(1 + drinks/day) on retirement status, birth year, and retirement status × birth year interaction and the logistic regression of response on log(1 + drinks/day) and retirement status[a]

| Variable | Parameters of linear regression | | | |
| | Without follow-ups | | With follow-ups | |
	Coefficient	Standard error	Coefficient	Standard error
Retirement status	0.384	0.170	0.299	0.165
Birth year	0.0172	0.00452	0.0127	0.00438
Retirement × birth year	− 0.0165	0.00757	− 0.0122	0.00734
Intercept	0.0253	0.0370	− 0.00085	0.0179
Root mean square error	0.572	0.0253	0.568	0.0144
	Parameters of logistic response			
Log(1 + drinks/day)	− 0.906	1.435	0.018	0.290
Retirement status	0.683	0.259	0.705	0.248
Intercept	2.608	0.475	2.472	0.103
	− Log likelihood = 1465.75		− Log likelihood = 1501.11	

[a] Parameters are constrained to lie between − 6 and 6.

variables in the model without follow-ups in Table 17 are more than twice as large as the corresponding coefficients in Table 16. This gives further evidence of the hazards in using the selection model without follow-ups.

Compared to the models fit without considering follow-ups, both models that take follow-ups into consideration had different estimates of the coefficients of the predictor variables in the linear regression. In the model summarized in Table 16, these estimates using follow-ups were larger in absolute value than the corresponding estimates disregarding follow-ups. In the model summarized in Table 17, these estimates using follow-ups were smaller in absolute value than the corresponding estimates disregarding follow-ups. There was a great deal of similarity in both the estimated coefficients and their standard errors between the two models fit using follow-ups. Neither of the models using follow-ups provided evidence for a strong influence of $\log(1 + \text{drinks/day})$ on response.

We also obtained estimates of the linear regression of $\log(1 + \text{drinks/day})$ on retirement status, birth year, and retirement status times birth year assuming a mixture model and multiply imputing the values of $\log(1 + \text{drinks/day})$ for the nonrespondents who were not followed up. Steps in this mixture modeling approach to estimation using follow-ups are summarized in Tables 18, 19, and 20, and final parameter estimates are shown in Table 21. Separate regressions were assumed to hold for respondents and nonrespondents and parameter estimates were those in Table 7. Five draws of regression parameters for nonrespondents were made and these are shown in Table 18. For each of the 74 nonrespondents who were not followed up and for each of these five drawn values of the nonrespondents' regression parameters, one value was drawn from the conditional distribution of $\log(1 + \text{drinks/day})$ given that individual's birth year and retirement status. If the drawn value of $\log(1 + \text{drinks/day})$ was less than zero, then it was set equal to zero. The five imputed values of each of the 74 nonrespondents who were not followed up are shown in Table 19. These imputed

Table 18. Five values of regression parameters for nonrespondents drawn from the distribution of these parameters given the regression among the 38 nonrespondent who were followed up

Parameter	Imputation number				
	1	2	3	4	5
Retirement status	−0.055	0.38	−0.10	−1.95	−1.03
Birth year	0.0036	−0.0034	0.0067	−0.088	−0.017
Retirement × birth year	−0.026	0.016	0.029	0.087	0.063
Intercept	−0.010	−0.13	−0.037	−0.104	−0.021
Root mean square error	0.51	0.55	0.59	0.58	0.60

Table 19. Five imputed values of log(1 + drinks/day) for each of the 74 nonrespondents who were not followed up

	Imputation number						Imputation number				
Number	1	2	3	4	5	Number	1	2	3	4	5
1	0.0	0.0	1.6	0.8	0.6	38	1.7	0.7	0.9	0.0	0.1
2	0.0	0.9	1.0	0.0	0.7	39	1.3	0.0	0.7	0.1	0.0
3	0.0	0.9	1.1	0.0	0.9	40	0.6	0.1	1.0	0.7	0.9
4	1.4	0.3	1.3	0.0	0.4	41	0.4	1.2	0.0	0.0	0.0
5	1.0	0.5	0.6	0.6	1.7	42	0.2	0.0	0.6	0.1	1.0
6	0.3	0.9	0.7	1.7	0.0	43	0.3	0.8	0.6	0.0	1.1
7	1.5	1.0	0.6	1.8	2.0	44	1.0	0.0	1.0	0.0	0.4
8	0.8	1.2	0.6	0.6	0.7	45	0.7	0.0	0.7	0.4	0.4
9	0.0	0.0	0.6	1.5	0.9	46	0.4	0.0	1.5	0.2	0.6
10	0.0	0.4	0.0	0.5	1.4	47	1.6	0.4	0.1	0.5	0.6
11	0.3	0.3	0.0	0.5	1.5	48	0.7	1.0	1.2	1.0	0.6
12	1.0	0.5	0.8	1.7	0.1	49	0.9	0.3	1.0	0.0	1.8
13	0.0	0.5	1.5	0.0	1.3	50	0.2	0.0	0.1	0.0	0.6
14	1.4	0.1	0.0	0.0	0.6	51	0.8	1.3	0.7	0.2	0.2
15	0.6	1.6	0.0	2.1	0.9	52	0.0	0.5	0.9	0.4	0.3
16	0.6	0.2	0.0	0.0	0.3	53	0.0	0.9	1.1	1.5	0.5
17	1.4	1.5	0.3	0.5	1.7	54	0.0	0.0	0.8	0.7	0.9
18	1.1	0.5	1.7	1.1	0.5	55	0.5	0.0	0.7	0.1	0.9
19	1.1	0.0	0.7	1.3	0.4	56	0.0	0.2	0.1	0.0	1.5
20	0.3	0.0	1.1	0.0	0.7	57	0.0	0.0	0.2	0.0	0.0
21	1.7	0.0	0.5	0.4	0.4	58	0.9	0.8	0.3	1.2	0.7
22	0.3	0.0	0.0	0.0	1.1	59	1.0	0.5	1.5	0.6	1.2
23	0.3	0.7	0.0	0.0	0.2	60	0.4	1.4	0.2	0.0	0.0
24	0.0	0.0	0.3	0.6	0.8	61	0.6	0.4	0.4	0.4	0.2
25	0.4	0.0	0.7	2.4	0.9	62	1.0	0.3	0.7	0.8	0.3
26	1.0	0.5	1.0	0.0	0.4	63	0.0	0.3	0.1	0.4	0.4
27	0.5	0.4	0.8	0.0	0.5	64	1.2	0.2	0.0	0.0	0.0
28	1.0	0.3	0.5	0.2	0.1	65	0.0	0.7	1.1	0.4	0.0
29	0.8	0.9	0.7	0.1	2.1	66	0.6	0.0	0.0	0.0	0.0
30	0.2	0.0	0.0	2.0	1.4	67	1.1	1.2	1.0	0.4	0.0
31	0.4	0.8	0.0	0.3	0.2	68	0.4	0.4	1.0	0.9	0.5
32	0.8	0.1	0.1	0.0	1.3	69	1.6	0.2	1.3	1.6	0.6
33	1.0	0.5	0.0	0.7	0.3	70	0.5	2.0	1.0	0.5	1.3
34	1.1	1.2	0.0	1.6	1.0	71	0.8	0.9	0.1	0.0	0.0
35	0.8	0.6	0.5	0.5	0.9	72	0.8	1.2	0.6	0.5	0.7
36	0.3	0.0	1.1	0.9	1.1	73	0.6	0.6	0.4	0.0	1.0
37	0.8	0.0	1.8	0.0	0.6	74	0.0	1.1	0.0	1.6	1.1

Table 20. Five sets of ordinary least squares regression coefficients from the five data sets with different imputed values of log(1 + drinks/day) for nonrespondents who were not followed up

	Imputation number				
Parameter	1	2	3	4	5
Retirement status	0.243	0.237	0.244	0.126	0.217
Birth year	0.0106	0.00953	0.01180	0.00594	0.01025
Retirement × birth year	−0.00907	−0.00854	−0.00917	−0.00420	−0.00790
Intercept	−0.00620	−0.0133	−0.00658	−0.01112	−0.00321
Root mean square error	0.565	0.567	0.565	0.574	0.567

Table 21. Multiple imputation estimates of the regression of log(1 + drinks/day) on retirement status, birth year and retirement status × birth year interaction[a]

Variable	Coefficient	Standard error	Percentage of missing information
Retirement status	0.213	0.168	9.1
Birth year	0.00962	0.00480	22.5
Retirement × birth year	−0.00778	0.00747	7.7
Intercept	−0.00809	0.0159	6.7
Root mean square error	0.568	—	—

[a]38 follow-ups are used to make 5 imputations for the 74 nonrespondents who are not followed up.

values were merged with the data for respondents and nonrespondents who were followed up to obtain five data sets with no missing data. Ordinary least squares regressions were performed on each of these five data sets. Table 20 shows the five sets of estimated regression coefficients. Regression coefficients shown in Table 21 are the mean of these five regression coefficients. These multiple imputation estimates were quite comparable to the estimates produced by the selection model approach using follow-ups. Estimated standard errors are also quite comparable between the two approaches.

IX. Summary

This report has indicated several difficulties with the selection model approach for the estimation of linear regression parameters when nonresponse depends on the outcome variable. When there are no covariates and the problem is to estimate the mean of a normally distributed outcome variable subject to nonignorable response, the joint likelihood of the normal distribution and the logistic response function is quite flat. Parameter estimates are thus unstable, and estimated standard errors based on asymptotic normal theory are large and unreliable. The approach is also sensitive to deviations from the assumed normal distribution. The same difficulties of a flat likelihood and sensitivity to the assumed normality will also occur in the extension of the approach to the estimation of linear regression parameters when all regressors are included as predictors of logistic response. Linear regression parameters will be much more sharply identified if there are predictors occurring in the linear regression which are not in the logistic response function, or predictors of response which are not related to the outcome. In practice it is essentially impossible to identify *a priori* a variable related to only one of response or outcome, and the results of Section VIII demonstrate that the linear regression estimates in practice can be quite sensitive to the specification of such a variable. The availability of outcome data on a sample of follow-ups makes the likelihood much more peaked, but estimation based on maximizing this likelihood is still sensitive to the assumed normality of residuals.

When there are no follow-ups available, the mixture model approach of Rubin (1977) requires more of the user than the selection model approach. The user must specify the relationship between the linear regression parameters among the respondents and these parameters among the nonrespondents. When a sample of follow-ups are available, these data may be used to directly estimate regression parameters among nonrespondents. Using the arguments of Rubin (1978) these estimated parameters can then be used to multiply impute values for nonrespondents who are not followed up. The mixture model approach is more robust to departures of residuals from normality than the selection model approach. Multiple imputation under the mixture model is also easier and cheaper to implement compared to the function maximization routines in BMDP used for the selection model approach. Computer costs for producing the mixture model estimates shown in Table 21 were about $5.00 compared to $15.00 for the computation of estimates shown in the two right-hand columns of Table 17.

Acknowledgments. Supported by the Medical Research Service of the Veterans Administration by NIH Grant GM 29745 and by NSF Grant SES 8311428.

Bibliography

Bergstrand, R., Vedin, A., Wilhelmsson, C., and Wilhelmsen, L. (1983). "Bias due to non-participation and heterogeneous sub-groups in population surveys." *J. Chron. Disease*, 36, 725–728.

Bossé, R., Ekerdt, D.J., and Silbert, J.E. (1984). "The Veterans Administration normative aging study." In S.A. Mednick, M. Harvey, and K.M. Finello (eds.), *Handbook of Longitudinal Research: Volume II. Teenage and Adult Cohorts.* New York: Praeger, 273–289.

Clark, W.B. and Midanik, L. (1982). "Alcohol use and alcohol problems among U.S. adults: Results of the 1979 national survey." In *Alcohol and Health Monograph No. 1, Alcohol Consumption and Related Problems*. Rockville, Maryland: National Institute of Alcohol Abuse and Alcoholism.

Cochran, W.G. (1977). *Sampling Techniques*, 3rd edn. New York: John Wiley.

Davis, P.J. and Rabinowitz, P. (1984). *Methods of Numerical Integration*, 2nd edn. Orlando, Florida: Academic Press.

de Lint, J. and Schmidt, W. (1976). "Alcohol and mortality." In B. Kissin and H. Begleiter (eds.), *The Biology of Alcoholism: Volume IV. Social Aspects of Alcoholism*. New York: Plenum, 275–305.

Dixon, W.J. (ed.) (1981). *BMDP Statistical Software 1981*. Berkeley: University of California Press.

Glynn, R.J., Bouchard, G.R., Locastro, J.S., and Laird, N.M. (1985). "Aging and generational effects on drinking behaviors in men: Results from the normative aging study." *Am. J. Public Health*, 75, 1413–1419.

Greenlees, J.S., Reece, W.S., and Zieschang, K.D. (1982). "Imputation of missing values when the probability of response depends on the variable being imputed." *J. Amer. Statist. Assoc.*, 77, 251–261.

Hansen, M.H. and Hurwitz, W.N. (1946). "The problem of nonresponse in sample surveys." *J. Amer. Statist. Assoc.*, 41, 517–529.

Heckman, J.J. (1974). "Shadow prices, market wages, and labor supply." *Econometrica*, 42, 679–694.

Heckman, J.J. (1976). "The common structure of statistical models of truncation, sample selection, and limited dependent variables and a simple estimator for such models." *Annals Econ. Soc. Meas.*, 5, 475–492.

Heckman, J.J. (1979). "Sample bias as a specification error." *Econometrica*, 47, 153–162.

Heckman, J.J. and Robb, R. (1985). "Alternative methods for evaluating the impact of interventions." In J.J. Heckman and B. Singer (eds.), *Longitudinal Analysis of Labor Market Data*. New York: Cambridge University Press.

Herzog, T.N. and Rubin, D.B. (1983). "Using multiple imputations to handle nonresponse in sample surveys." In W.G. Madow, I. Olkin, and D.B. Rubin (eds.), *Incomplete Data in Sample Surveys, Volume 2. Theory and Bibliographies*. New York: Academic Press, 209–245.

International Mathematical and Statistical Libraries (1982). "Zeros and extrema; linear programming." In *International Mathematical and Statistical Libraries 9*. Houston: International Mathematical and Statistical Libraries Inc.

Lee, L.F. (1979). "Identification and estimation in binary choice models with limited (censored) dependent variables." *Econometrica*, 47, 977–996.

Little, R.J.A. (1982). "Models for nonresponse in sample surveys." *J. Amer. Statist. Assoc.*, 77, 237–250.

Murnane, R.J., Newstead, S., and Olsen, R.J. (1985). "Comparing public and private schools: The puzzling role of selectivity bias." *J. Bus. Econ. Statist.*, 3, 23–35.

Okafor, R. (1982). *Bias Due to Logistic Nonresponse in Sample Surveys*. Ph.D. thesis. Cambridge, Massachusetts: Harvard University.

Olsen, R.L. (1980). "A least squares correction for selectivity bias." *Econometrica*, 48, 1815–1820.

Rubin, D.B. (1977). "Formalizing subjective notions about the effect of nonrespondents in sample surveys." *J. Amer. Statist. Assoc.*, 72, 538–543.

Rubin, D.B. (1978). "Multiple imputations in sample surveys—A phenomenological Bayesian approach to nonresponse." In *Imputation and Editing of Faulty or Missing Data*. Washington, D.C.: U.S. Department of Commerce, Social Security Administration.

Rubin, D.B. (1985). *Multiple Imputation for Nonresponse*. New York: John Wiley.

SAS Institute. (1982). *SAS User's Guide: Basics*. Cary, North Carolina: SAS Institute.

Discussion 4: Mixture Modeling Versus Selection Modeling with Nonignorable Nonresponse

DISCUSSANT: JOHN W. TUKEY

Let me make one terminological remark. I'd like to encourage Don to use a different word than "multiple" because that word leaves me expecting something else. I think "repeated" or "parallel" or something of that sort would be a more helpful term. You were just now saying that you would like to do this for more than one set, one model, one structure. I think that's where the word multiple comes in. You need a more "withiny" sort of word for doing it over and over in the same frame. Is "multiple" in printed papers yet?

DON RUBIN: Yes, I use it to refer to both the between model and within model variation in values, but I can try to use "repeated" or "parallel" to refer to within model variation and use "multiple," as now, to refer to both.

JOHN TUKEY: You could at least consider modification. You see the point. If my Bayesian calibrations were as good as some other people, maybe I would know how much I wanted to trust the results of this. But it seems to me that you've illustrated in a real example—it doesn't say that it always happens—that the sort of standard errors you get with this process are as large as you get by other processes. That makes me quite susceptible to the arguments about simplicity and about staying closer to the data. Since I never expect to be able to tell a client what's the best thing to do, I wouldn't know what to say to a client in the way of a change, at the moment, for somebody who was doing the parallel imputations. I hope in 20 years we might know something even better, but I wouldn't necessarily want to bet on it. In other words, I'm saying you leave me moderately convinced that this is the state-of-the-art.

JOHN HARTIGAN: I think it's interesting to discover techniques that don't work, like the selection models that you discuss, because you can often learn things by trying to find out exactly how they don't work. I also think that, when one works with Bayesian theory, one often finds that a lot of theoretical results say, "If you do this or that Bayesian thing, you get pretty much the same as some other classical thing." That's how almost all theoretical Bayesian results go. So I always like to see examples where, if you do this or that Bayesan thing, you get something pretty different from classical things. I think, after all, those are the cases where Bayes' theory will stand or fall: the cases where they suggest doing different things. I

believe that those cases are like the essence of nonrobustness. They are
cases where the probability distributions that you assume have a large effect
on your conclusion and they cannot be tested by the data. I believe that this
problem is one like that. It's a problem where I think that the probabilistic
description you get at first is entirely the right one. In the simplest form,
you have a categorical variable R which takes the values 1 or 0 and a
response variable Y, which is a real-valued variable. The observations you
actually have in hand consist of a series of values of R, which all happen to
be 1, and the corresponding values of Y. Now I think when it is explained
in those bold terms, most people will realize that something is missing from
this data set. What's missing are the values of Y when $R = 0$. I felt Don
was cheating just a little bit in solving this problem by introducing some
cases where $R = 0$ because, when you introduce some follow-up cases
(especially when you assume it's a random sample) you reduce it back to
standard problems. You've now got observations! It's true that maybe the
proportions are different, so you have to weight the proportions, but you
can reduce it back to a standard problem. If you want to look at the hard,
nasty, nasty problem, it probably is a good idea not to give yourself the
benefit of knowledge, that is, the benefit of actually knowing the nonresponse. What do you do when indeed R is equal to 0? I really do believe
that if you consult what you do when $R = 0$, you would find that the two
approaches (the selection model approach and the mixture model approach)
have to be the same. After all, if you've got to specify a probability model,
then there's a joint probability model for R and Y. One way of doing it is a
selection model. In the selection model you say that you know the conditional distribution of R given Y and you know the distribution of R
because you have observed how many nonrespondents there are. So, clearly
you know the joint distribution of R and Y in the selection model. In the
mixture model you say you know the conditional distribution of Y given R
and again you know the distribution of R. Thus, again you've got to know
the joint distribution of Y and R. If I want to compare the two approaches,
I would look at the joint distribution of Y and R; if they have the same
joint distributions, you have to have the same final answers.

I think that you're getting different answers because you're making
different kinds of probability assumptions about the missing parts. In the
Bayesian approach that you're discussing, you're more forthrightly coming
in with the missing part of the data saying, "This is the hard part. When R
is equal to 0, we assume the distribution is so and so." But, I think you will
agree, that if you're really ignorant about the $R = 0$ case, you're going to
have a huge variability in the conclusions you draw about the means of
those underlying distributions. I suspect that the part of the variability in
your conclusions that depends on the particular assumptions about $R = 0$ is
what corresponds, in the selection model case, to the fact that the likelihood
function is so flat. Because the likelihood function is flat means that it just

can't tell where those parameters are. In the selection model case you've got all the parameters in there at once and so it has to come through and say, "I really don't know." You could probably take an integrated approach to this. Looking at the joint distributions, there must be a correspondence between the two models. They have to come together, so you could probably work out the relationship between the level of assumptions. I believe, just for simplicity of analysis, you should ask what you would do without followups.

DON RUBIN: Let me respond to John Hartigan first. Both the selection modeling approach and the mixture modeling approach specify a joint distribution for Y and R (given X), but the parametric structure is different. The selection model approach specifies (i) a model for Y given parameter θ_Y and (ii) a model for R given Y and parameter $\theta_{R|Y}$, where θ_Y and $\theta_{R|Y}$ are *a priori* independent. The mixture model approach specifies (i) a model for Y given R and parameter $\theta_{Y|R}$ and (ii) a model for R given parameter θ_R where $\theta_{Y|R}$ and θ_R are *a priori* independent. My argument is just that if you specify things the selection modeling way, then the sensitivity to the fact that you don't have any Y values when $R = 0$ is more difficult to see. What you don't know gets combined with what you do.

Whereas with mixture modeling approach you are confronted with it immediately. One part is easy to estimate: it's just the binomial for R. The second part is a product with two pieces; over $R = 1$ people and over $R = 0$ people. For the $R = 1$ people it's easy; for the $R = 0$ people, it's hard. There are no data there. You're just hit in the face with that. Consequently, if you're going to do any sort of inference about the parameters that you want (θ_Y, the parameters of the distribution), you must make some assumptions about what this conditional distribution of Y given $R = 0$ is like. I think that the way you make those assumptions is to be direct and very simple.

I took this approach in my 1977 paper (Rubin, 1977; *JASA*, p. 538), which does exactly what you asked for about outcomes without followups. The idea there is to suppose that we make the spread of these unknown priors wider and wider to see when you no longer get an answer that's acceptable. You can see a range of answers. Do answers only break down at some point where the difference between the respondents and the nonrespondents is so large that it is beyond what could be believed? I'm saying, do a sensitivity analysis and see what the answers are.

With a selection model such a sensitivity analysis is much harder to do. You have to specify a different distributional structure for Y; maybe it's the Box–Cox family, maybe it's something else. It's all tainted. The idea is the same as when you try to estimate parameters and find some parameters are very well estimated so the likelihood is steep in some directions, but it is flat in other directions. A useful thing to do is to find what are those directions.

JOHN HARTIGAN: My point is, Don, I think we both appreciate that these are both joint distributions. Thus, in the final analysis you want the model to specify a joint distribution. Both models specify a joint distribution. Anything you do one way with a Bayesian analysis must translate into a specific selection model.

DON RUBIN: No, not if I make the assumption that these parameters are independent. They're tied together in different ways. I'm talking about specific models. I'm not saying what they could be if you generalize them beyond what they are now. We both understand what the issue is. I'm talking about two applied tools that exist, how they're used, and what assumptions are always attached to them. They're different.

JOHN HARTIGAN: I want to start off with your mixture model and go to the selection model. Let's start off with a mixture model of normals that had one representing $R = 0$ and the other $R = 1$. In fact, let's make it easy and consider classical discrimination. Now let's translate this into a simple selection model analysis in which we first work out the distribution of Y. What will the distribution of Y be given a mixture of normals? What will the distribution of R given Y be? It will be a logistic distribution.

DON RUBIN: But the parameters are tied together in a different way than if you started with the mixture of normals as being the distributional form and had *a priori* independent parameters for the logistic regression. They're wound together.

JOHN HARTIGAN: That's not necessarily so.

DON RUBIN: You make a theoretical point which I agree with. But the way the world now operates, using the two models, gives a difference.

JOHN HARTIGAN: The selection model is the same as the mixture model because they both describe the joint distribution of the thing.

DON RUBIN: Then we should throw out both terms because there's no use in having them. I'm using them to describe different things and so I've made this distinction about the parameters. I'd rather have two terms to use to describe two different things that are being done. You're making the point, which is perfectly valid, that these two things are not different in some general world. I completely agree that they're not different in principle, but they are different in practice, and I am using the terms to describe the practice of them.

PAUL HOLLAND: Is the likelihood that you would get from the selection models a truly different creature than the one that would occur with a mixture model?

DON RUBIN: I don't know quite what you mean. They're both likelihoods, but the parameter space factors in different ways for the two models.

EDITOR'S COMMENT: **The parameter space does indeed factor in quite a different way. Holland explored this subsequent to the conference. His result, with a modification that Tukey suggested, is included as an addendum to this discussion.**

COMMENT FROM AUDIENCE: It occurs to me that the selection model has a psychological interpretation that is lacking in a mixture model. Suppose in running a survey, I decided to pay $10 per response rather than $1—that would raise the response rate in a selection model with a selection function. With a mixture model it doesn't work as well.

DON RUBIN: Absolutely. I am not saying that selection models should not be used to think about problems. I'm talking about a narrow point that perhaps I ought to clear up. This technique (maximum likelihood with a selection model) as used, I don't regard as a good, applied tool. I regard the other one (mixture modeling) as a good, applied tool. Thinking about factoring distributions is a great way to build models. The more modeling tricks we have up our sleeves, the better we are able to map these formal models into reality. In many cases it's natural to think about the selection part of it and that's very useful for building models.

Thus, if we're looking to see what would be a reasonable range of distributions or values to use in the multiple imputation scheme, I might be very happy using some sort of selection model, if I thought it was close to reality. This might help me get some idea of what kind of model to start with; that would bound the range of models in some way. But I don't think, after this initial structuring, that this maximum-likelihood-estimated selection model is a good thing to use.

QUESTION FROM AUDIENCE: You talked about just a marginal prior distribution on the parameters of the nonrespondents. Don't you also have to introduce a conditional prior on how the nonrespondent parameters differed from the respondent parameters? If you do have to introduce that, doesn't that represent a strong assumption? Won't your results be affected by that assumption?

DON RUBIN: With follow-ups you don't have to put in any sort of informative prior. The paper in *JASA* in 1977 deals exactly with how to specify a conditional prior distribution of the nonrespondents' parameters given the respondents' parameters.

QUESTION FROM AUDIENCE: That's not explained in this paper?

DON RUBIN: Only in one table where the prior is Normal $(-0.3, 0.3)$, just to illustrate that it doesn't make much difference when you have follow-ups. It's a very minor part of what's being done here. But you're absolutely right. You have to specify that conditional prior distribution. That's what drives the whole estimation process when there are no follow-ups. It's what hooks up the data on the respondents to the parameter for the nonrespondents. What I did in the 1977 paper was to try to formulate that prior in such a way that made it easy for applied people, in this case people at ETS and people at the Office of Education to speculate, "Are these reasonable ranges of parameters. Do I expect things to change that much?"

QUESTION FROM AUDIENCE: Didn't you assume in that paper that nonresponse parameters are centered around the respondents with no bias term?

DON RUBIN: Yes, but because in that application, that was considered a reasonable assumption. After adjusting for the covariates, the researchers didn't know why the missing responses would be biased one way or the other way. In the current case, for example, are we expecting the nonrespondents to drink more or less than respondents of the same age? If you don't know whether it should be more or less, then you should center the adjustment at zero and spread it out. Some of the coefficients generated during this Monte Carlo technique will be positive, indicating they are drinking more. Some will be negative, indicating they are drinking less. The bias will go back and forth yielding an interval that reflects the uncertainty about how much you know about how much more or less they might be drinking.

COMMENT FROM AUDIENCE: I've had a hard time getting people to specify these conditional distributions. I can't get the kind of agreement that you got in that paper. People don't believe what I'm saying. One person might say one thing and I'll get one kind of result. Another provides a different prior and I get an entirely different set of results. My clients get the feeling that this is very subjective.

DON RUBIN: That's probably because of the kind of data you have. If the answers move around that much, then that's the answer. You can't nail down the answer without getting better information. That's what I mean by "being honest." If you don't know the answer, don't give a point estimate and walk away. The fact is that you can't get agreement. All the parameters that are being generated under these procedures are plausible values, and the values that are being imputed are plausible, and yet the inference goes all over the place. But that's life and your answer.

COMMENT FROM AUDIENCE (CONTINUED): My general point was that you criticized selection modeling because it makes strong assumptions and the results are not robust with respect to those assumptions. But I get the feeling that your approach also makes assumptions. They're more in the form of certain kinds of beliefs about how the parameters underlying the nonrespondent distribution differ from the parameters underlying the respondent distribution. But your results also may be sensitive to those assumptions. I wonder just how assumption free mixture modeling really is.

DON RUBIN: No, it's not assumption free. The procedure is designed to *expose* the uncertainty. It's designed to expose the sensitivity to the assumptions, to a range of assumptions. The whole point is trying to show how the answers might change with the parameters governing how much you think that respondents and nonrespondents differ. You can see it if, for the values you're generating, the answers go all over the map; then mixture modeling has exposed that uncertainty. The aim of mixture modeling is not to come up with just one estimate, which seems to be the aim with selection modeling. And with follow-up data, the mixture modeling approach does just as well as the selection modeling approach when the specified selection model is basically true, and better when the specified selection model is inaccurate.

A Comment on Remarks by Rubin and Hartigan

PAUL W. HOLLAND

Consider the following simplified setting of the problem discussed by Dr. Rubin. (Y, R) have a joint distribution over a population of units in which Y is a variable of interest and $R = 0$ for a unit if it is a nonrespondent and $R = 1$ otherwise. Dr. Rubin considers the problem of specifying the joint distribution of (Y, R) and distinguishes two methods of doing this:

(M) Mixture model: specify $Y|R$ and R,
(S) Selection model: specify $R|Y$ and Y.

In (M) we specify the two conditional densities $f_1(y)$ and $f_0(y)$ for $Y|R = 1$ and $Y|R = 0$ respectively; also the marginal respondent proportion, $p = P(R = 1)$. In (S) we specify the *selection function*

$$r(y) = P(R = 1|Y = y)$$

and the marginal distribution of Y whose density we denote by

$$g(y).$$

The virtue of (M) is that it is perfectly clear that $f_0(y)$ is completely undetermined, unidentified, and unobserved. However, as Hartigan's discussion points out, any uncertainty expressed by (M) should also appear somewhere in (S). The purpose of this comment is to show just how the unidentifiability of $f_0(y)$ shows up in $r(y)$ and $g(y)$.

It is clear that the basic elements of (M), which are p, $f_1(y)$ and $f_0(y)$, can be expressed in terms of the basic elements of (S), which are $r(y)$ and $g(y)$. The equations are

$$p = \int r(y)g(y)\,dy \tag{1}$$

$$f_1(y) = \frac{r(y)g(y)}{p} \tag{2}$$

$$f_0(y) = \frac{[1 - r(y)]g(y)}{1 - p}. \tag{3}$$

Hence, we see the remarkable fact that while the product

$$r(y)g(y) \tag{4}$$

is identifiable (i.e., can be estimated with arbitrary precision as long as there are enough data), the very similar product

$$[1 - r(y)]g(y) \tag{5}$$

is completely unidentifiable. No amount of data can tell us anything about the function in Equation (5). I find the identifiability of $r(y)g(y)$ coupled with the complete unidentifiability of the very similar product $[1 - r(y)]g(y)$ to be rather amazing. It certainly shows how the no-free-lunch principle can show up in weird ways.

Hence, just as $f_0(y)$ in (M) must come from prior knowledge or simply remain an unknown that we may manipulate in a sensitivity analysis, so too must the product of $1 - r(y)$ and $g(y)$ in (S).

One might use Equations (2) and (3) to see if choices of $r(y)$ and $g(y)$ obtained from a selection model are reasonable in terms of their implied values for f_1 and f_0.

We can reverse the process, of course, and solve for $r(y)$ and $g(y)$ in terms of p, $f_1(y)$, and $f_0(y)$. The equations are

$$r(y) = \frac{pf_1(y)}{g(y)} \tag{6}$$

$$g(y) = pf_1(y) + (1 - p)f_0(y). \tag{7}$$

Equations (6) and (7) also show how the arbitrariness of $f_0(y)$ propagates into $g(y)$ and $r(y)$. For example, if $1 - p$ is small, then the effect of variation in f_0 can be limited. The logit of $r(y)$ is interesting since it is a way that selection functions can be specified. The logit of $r(y)$, $\lambda(y)$, is given by

$$\lambda(y) = \log\left(\frac{r(y)}{1 - r(y)}\right) = \log\left(\frac{p}{1 - p}\right) + \log f_1(y) - \log f_0(y). \tag{8}$$

In Equation (8) we see that the uncertainty of the f_0 propagates rather dramatically into $\lambda(y)$. Virtually all of the dependence of $\lambda(y)$ on y is determined by an unknowable function, f_0! It is difficult for me, personally, to see how strong confidence could be placed in any *a priori* choice of selection function, $r(y)$, in view of Equation (8).

I am sure all of this extends to the cases of interest to Heckman in which there are both independent *and* dependent variables, but I do not think that the problems raised here get better in that setting. It is always potentially dangerous to speculate without data, but perhaps Equations (2) and (3) can help the selection modelers check on the reasonableness of their speculations from a different point of view.

In reacting to the above observations, John Tukey noted that the methods used to decompose the joint distribution of (Y, R) by (M) and (S) are not the only ones possible. He suggests a model based on specifying the two conditional distributions, i.e.,

(SS) Simplified selection model: specify $R|Y$ and $Y|R = 1$.

In (SS) we specify the *selection function* $r(y)$ as in (S), but we only specify the identifiable distribution $f_1(y)$ as in (M) rather than specifying $g(y)$ as in (S). Equation (8) can then be rewritten as

$$f_0(y) = \frac{p}{1-p} \frac{1-r(y)}{r(y)} f_1(y) \qquad (9)$$

so that the unidentifiable $f_0(y)$ is now expressed in terms of the specified elements of (SS), $f_1(y)$, and $r(y)$—the value of p is simply determined in Equation (9) by normalizing the integral of $f_0(y)$ to unity. The unidentifiability of $f_0(y)$ now is seen to be the unidentifiability of $r(y)$ while $f_1(y)$ remains identifiable. Tukey's way of specifying a selection model has the advantage of dealing with $f_1(y)$, which can be estimated easily, and with $r(y)$, which is potentially easy to think about. Equation (9) can then be used to see the implication for $f_0(y)$ of any choice of $r(y)$ and estimate of $f_1(y)$.

Bibliography

Action Committee Against Narcotics. (1981). *Hong Kong Narcotics Report.*

Amemiya, T. (1981). "Qualitative response models: A survey." *J. Econ. Lit.*, 19, 1483–1536.

Ashenfelter, O. (1978). "Estimating the effect of training programs on earnings." *Rev. Econ. Statist.*, 60, 47–57.

Astin, A. (1971). *Predicting Academic Performance in College.* New York: Free Press.

Barnow, B., Cain, G., and Goldberger, A. (1980). "Issues in the analysis of selectivity bias." In E. Stromsdorfer and G. Farkas (eds.), *Evaluation Studies*, vol. 5. San Francisco: Sage.

Barros, R. (1986). *Three Essays on Selection and Identification Problems in Economics.* Ph.D. thesis. University of Chicago, Chicago, Illinois.

Bassi, L. (1983). *Estimating the Effect of Training Programs with Nonrandom Selection.* Ph.D. thesis. Princeton University, Princeton, New Jersey.

Bergstrand, R., Vedin, A., Wilhelmsson, C., and Wilhelmsen, L. (1983). Bias due to non-participation and heterogeneous sub-groups in population surveys." *J. Chron. Disease*, 36, 725–728.

Blalock, H.M. (1961). *Causal Inferences in Nonexperimental Research.* Chapel Hill: University of North Carolina Press.

Bosse, R., Ekerdt, D.J., and Silbert, J.E. (1984). "The Veterans Administration normative aging study." In S.A. Mednick, M. Harvey, and K.M. Finello (eds.), *Handbook of Longitudinal Research: Volume II. Teenage and Adult Cohorts.* New York: Praeger, 273–289.

Brook, R.C. and Whitehead, P.C. (1980). *Drug-Free Therapeutic Community.* New York: Human Sciences Press.

Chamberlain, G. (1982). "Multivariate regression models for panel data." *J. Econometrics*, 18, 1–46.

Chase, C. and Barritt, L. (1966). "A table of concordance between ACT and SAT." *J. College Student Pers.*, 8, 105–108.

Clark, W.B. and Midanik, L. (1982). "Alcohol use and alcohol problems among U.S. adults: Results of the 1979 national survey." In *Alcohol and Health Monograph No. 1, Alcohol Consumption and Related Problems.* Rockville, Maryland: National Institute of Alcohol Abuse and Alcoholism.

Cochran, (1957). "Analysis of covariance: Its nature and uses." *Biometrics*, 13, 261–281.

Cochran, W.G. (1977). *Sampling Techniques*, 3rd edn. New York: John Wiley.

Coleman, J.C. (1985). "Schools, families and children." Ryerson Lecture, University of Chicago, Chicago, Illinois, April 1985.

Cox, D.R. (1985). *The Planning of Experiments*. New York: John Wiley.

Davis, P.J. and Rabinowitz, P. (1984). *Methods of Numerical Integration*, 2nd edn. Orlando, Florida: Academic Press.

Dawid, A.P. (1979). "Conditional independence in statistical theory (with discussion)." *J. Roy. Statist. Soc. Ser. B*, 41, 1–31.

De Lint, J. and Schmidt, W. (1976). "Alcohol and mortality." In B. Kissin and H. Begleiter (eds.), *The Biology of Alcoholism: Volume IV. Social Aspects of Alcoholism*. New York: Plenum, 275–305.

Dixon, W.J., ed. (1981). *BMDP Statistical Software 1981*. Berkeley: University of California Press.

Dole, V.P. (1972a). "Comments on 'heroin maintenance'." *J. Amer. Med. Assoc.*, 220, 1493.

Dole, V.P. (1972b). "Detoxification of sick addicts in prison." *J. Amer. Med. Assoc.*, 220, 366–369.

Dole, V.P. (1980). "Addictive behavior." *Scient. Amer.*, 243, 138–154.

Dole, V.P. and Joseph, H. (1979). *Long Term Consequences of Methadone Maintenance Treatment*. New York: Community Treatment Foundation. (Final report under Contract 5 H81 DA 01778-02.)

Dole, V.P. and Nyswander, M.E. (1965). "A medical treatment for diacetylmorphine (heroin) addiction." *J. Amer. Med. Assoc.*, 193, 646–650.

Dole, V.P. and Nyswander, M.E. (1968). "Methadone maintenance and its implications for theories of heroin addiction." In *The Addictive States*. Association for Research in Nervous and Mental Disease, Vol. XLVI, 359–366.

Dole, V.P. and Singer, B. (1979). "On the evaluation of treatments for narcotics addiction." *J. Drug Issues*, 9(2), 205–211.

Dole, V.P., Nyswander, M.E., and Kreek, M.J. (1966). "Narcotic Blockade." *Arch. Intern. Med.*, 118, 304–309.

Dole, V.P., Nyswander, M.E., DesJarlais, D., and Joseph, H. (1982). "Performance-based ratings of methadone maintenance programs." *New England J. Med.*, 306, 169–172.

DuPont, R.L. (1971). "Profiles of a heroin-addiction epidemic." *New England J. Med.*, 285(6), 320–324.

Feinstein, A. (1985). *Clinical Epidemiology*. Philadelphia: W.B. Saunders.

Fienberg, S., Singer, B., and Tanur, J. (1985). "Large-scale social experimentation in the United States." In A.C. Atkinson and S. Fienberg (eds.), *A Celebration of Statistics*. Berlin/New York: Springer-Verlag.

Finney, D.J. (1984). "Improvement by planned multistage selection." *J. Amer. Statist. Assoc.*, 79(387), 501–509.

Fisher, R.A. (1953). *The Design of Experiments*. London: Hafner.

Glynn, R.J., Bouchard, G.R., Locastro, J.S., and Laird, N.M. (in press). "Aging and generational effects on drinking behaviors in men: Results from the normative aging study."

Goldfeld, S. and Quandt, R. (1976). "Techniques for estimating switching regressions." In S. Goldfeld and R. Quandt (eds.), *Studies in Nonlinear Estimation*. Cambridge, Massachusetts: Ballinger.

Greenlees, J.S., Reece, W.S., and Zieschang, K.D. (1982). "Imputation of missing values when the probability of response depends on the variable being imputed." *J. Amer. Statist. Assoc.*, 77, 251–261.

Gunne, L.-M. (1983). "The case of the Swedish methadone maintenance treatment program." *Drug and Alcohol Dependence*, 11, 99–103.

Gunne, L.-M. and Gronbladh, L. (1981). "A Swedish methadone maintenance program: A controlled study." *Drug and Alcohol Dependence*, 7, 249–256.

Hansen, M.H. and Hurwitz, W.N. (1946). "The problem of nonresponse in sample surveys." *J. Amer. Statist. Assoc.*, 41, 517–529.

Heckman, J. (1974). "Shadow prices, market wages, and labor supply." *Econometrica*, 42, 679–694.

Heckman, J. (1976). "The common structure of statistical models of truncation, sample selection, limited dependent variables and a simple estimator for such models." *Annals Econ. Soc. Meas.*, 5, 475–492.

Heckman, J. (1976). "Simultaneous equations models with continuous and discrete endogenous variables and structural shifts." In S. Goldfeld and R. Quandt (eds.), *Studies in Nonlinear Estimation*. Cambridge, Massachusetts: Ballinger.

Heckman, J. (1978). "Dummy endogenous variables in a simultaneous equations system." *Econometrica*, 46, 931–961.

Heckman, J. (1979). "Sample selection bias as a specification error." *Econometrica*, 47, 153–161.

Heckman, J. (1980). "Addendum to sample selection bias as a specification error." In E. Stromsdorfer and G. Farkas (eds.), *Evaluation Studies*, vol. 5. San Francisco: Sage.

Heckman, J. and Neumann, G. (1977). "Union wage differentials and the decision to join unions." Unpublished manuscript, University of Chicago, Chicago, Illinois.

Heckman, J. and Robb, R. (1985). "Alternative methods for evaluating the impact of interventions." In J. Heckman and B. Singer (eds.), *Longitudinal Analysis of Labor Market Data*. New York: Cambridge University Press.

Heckman, J. and Wolpin, K. (1976). "Does the contract compliance program work?: An analysis of Chicago data." *Indust. Labor Relations Rev.*, 19, 415–433.

Herzog, T.N. and Rubin. D.B. (1983). "Using multiple imputations to handle nonresponse in sample surveys." In W.G. Madow, I. Olkin, and D.B. Rubin (eds.), *Incomplete Data in Sample Surveys, Volume 2. Theory and Bibliographies*. New York: Academic Press, 209–245.

International Mathematical and Statistical Libraries. (1982). "Zeros and extrema; linear programming." In *International Mathematical and Statistical Libraries 9*. Houston: International Mathematical and Statistical Libraries Inc.

Koopmans, T.C., Rubins, H., and Leipnik, R.B. (1950). "Measuring the equation systems of dynamic economics." In T.C. Koopmans (ed.), *Statistical Inference in Dynamic Economic Models, Cowles Commission Monograph 10*. New York: John Wiley.

Lee, L.F. (1978). "Unionism and wage rates: A simultaneous equations model with qualitative and limited dependent variables." *Intl. Econ. Rev.*, 19, 415–433.

Lee, L.F. (1979). "Identification and estimation in binary choice models with limited (censored) dependent variables." *Econometrica*, 47, 977–996.

Little, R.J. (1982). "Models for nonresponse in sample surveys." *J. Amer. Statist. Assoc.*, 77, 237–250.

Little, R.J. (1985). "A note about models for selectivity bias." *Econometrica*, 53(6), 1469–1474.

MaCurdy, T. (1982). "The use of time series processes to model the error structure of earnings in a longitudinal data analysis." *J. Econometrics*, 18(1), 83–114.

Manski, C. and Lerman, S. (1977). "The estimation of choice probabilities from choice-based samples." *Econometrica*, 45, 1977–1988.

Manski, C. and McFadden, D. (1981). "Alternative estimators and sample designs for discrete choice analysis." In C. Manski and D. McFadden (eds.), *Structural Analysis of Discrete Data with Econometric Applications*. Cambridge, Massachusetts: MIT Press.

Mundlak, Y. (1961). "Empirical production functions free of management bias." *J. Farm Econometrics*, 43, 45–56.

Mundlak, Y. (1978). "On the pooling of time series and cross section data." *Econometrica*, 46, 69–85.

Murnane, R.J., Newstead, S., and Olsen, R.J. (1985). "Comparing public and private schools: The puzzling role of selectivity bias." *J. Bus. Econ. Statist.*, 3, 23–35.

Newman, R.G. (1977). *Methadone Treatment in Narcotic Addiction.* New York: Academic Press.

Newman, R.G. (1984). "Testimony before the Senate Subcommittee on Alcoholism and Drug Abuse." 98th Congress, 2nd Session, Committee on Labor and Human Resources, United States Senate, S.HRG. 98-778, 44–60.

Newman, R.G. and Whitehall, W.B. (1979). "Double-blind comparison of methadone and placebo maintenance treatments of narcotics addicts in Hong Kong." *Lancet*, 2, 485–488.

Newman, R.G., Tytum, A., and Bashkow, S. (1976). "Retention of patients in the York City Methadone Maintenance Treatment Program." *Int. J. Addictions*, 11, 905–931.

Okafor, R. (1982). *Bias Due to Logistic Nonresponse in Sample Surveys.* Ph.D. thesis. Cambridge, Massachusetts: Harvard University.

Olsen, R.L. (1980). "A least squares correction for selectivity bias." *Econometrica*, 48, 1815–1820.

Olsson, B., Carlsson, G., Fant, M. Johansson, T., Olsson, O., and Roth, C. (1981). "Heavy drug abuse in Sweden 1979—A national case-finding study in Sweden." *Drug and Alcohol Dependence*, 7, 273–283.

Page, E.B. and Feifs, H. (1985). "SAT scores and American states: Seeking for useful meaning." *J. Ed. Meas.*, 21(1).

Powell, B. and Steelman, L.C. (1984). "Variations in state SAT performance: Meaningful or misleading?" *Harvard Ed. Rev.*, 54, 389–412.

Pugh, R. and Sassenrath, J. (1968). "Comparable scores for the CEEB Scholastic Aptitude Test and the American College Test program." *Meas. Eval. Guid.*, 1, 103–109.

Ramist, L. and Arbeiter, S. (1984). *Profiles, College-bound Seniors*, 1983. New York: The College Board.

Robins, L.N., Helzer, J.E., and Davis, D.H. (1975). "Narcotic use in southeast Asia and afterward." *Arch. Gen. Psychiatry*, 32, 955–961.

Rosenbaum, P. (1984). "The consequences of adjustment for a concomitant variable that has been effected by the treatment." *J. Roy. Statist. Soc. Ser. A*, 147, 656–666.

Rosenbaum, P. and Rubin, D. (1983). "The central role of the propensity score in observational studies for causal effects." *Biometrika*, 70, 41–55.

Rosenbaum, P. and Rubin, D. (1985). "Constructing a control group using multivariate sampling methods that incorporate the propensity score." *Amer. Statist.*, 39(1), 33–38.

Roy, A. (1951). "Some thoughts on the distribution of earnings." *Oxford Econ. Pap.*, 3, 135–146.

Rubin, D.B. (1977). "Formalizing subjective notions about the effects of nonrespondents in sample surveys." *J. Amer. Statist. Assoc.*, 72, 538–543.

Rubin, D.B. (1978). "Multiple imputations in sample surveys—A phenomenological Bayesian approach to nonresponse." In *Imputation and Editing of Faulty or Missing Data*. Washington, D.C.: U.S. Department of Commerce, Social Security Adminstration.

Rubin, D.B. (1985). *Multiple Imputation for Nonresponse*. New York: John Wiley.

SAS Institute. (1982). *SAS User's Guide: Basics.* Cary, North Carolina: SAS Institute.

Scheuren, F. (1985). "Evaluating manpower training: Some notes on data handling issues." Report to JTLS Panel, U.S. Department of Labor, Washington, D.C.

Simon, H. (1957a). "Spurious correlation: A casual interpretation." In H. Simon (ed.), *Models of Man*. New York: John Wiley, 37–49.

Simon, H. (1957b). "Causal ordering and identifiability." In H. Simon (ed.), *Models of Man*. New York: John Wiley.

Steelman, L.C. and Powell, B. (1985). "Appraising the implications of the AST for educational policy." *Phi Delta Kappan*, 603–606.

Vaillant, G.E. (1966a). "A 12 year follow-up of New York narcotic addicts: I. The relation of treatment to outcome." *Amer. J. Psychiatry*, 122, 727–737.

Vaillant, G.E. (1966b). "A 12 year follow-up of New York narcotic addicts: II. The natural history of a chronic disease." *New England J. Med.*, 275, 1282–1288.

Vaillant, G.E. (1966c). "A 12 year follow-up of New York narcotic addicts: III. Some social and psychiatric characteristics." *Arch. Gen. Psychiatry*, 15, 599–606.

Vaillant, G.E. (1966d). "A 12 year follow-up of New York narcotic addicts: IV. Some determinants and characteristics of abstinence." *Amer. J. Psychiatry*, 123, 573–584.

Vaillant, G.E. (1973). "A 20 year follow-up of New York narcotic addicts." *Arch. Gen. Psychiatry*, 29, 237–241.

Wainer, H. (1986). "Five pitfalls encountered while trying to compare states on their SAT scores." *J. Ed. Meas.*, 23, 69–81.

Wainer, H., Holland, P.W., Swinton, S., and Wang, M. (1985). "On State Education Statistics." *J. Ed. Statist.*, 10, 293–325.

Working, E.J. (1927). "What do statistical 'demand curves' show?" *Quart. J Econ.*, 41(1).

Author Index

Subject Index